Your Towns and Cities ir

Salisbury
in the Great War

DEDICATION

To my grandchildren.
May they never suffer a repeat of the calamity enshrined
in this narrative.

Your Towns and Cities in the Great War

Salisbury
in the Great War

Neil G.M. Hall

Pen & Sword
MILITARY

First published in Great Britain in 2016 by
PEN & SWORD MILITARY
an imprint of
Pen and Sword Books Ltd
47 Church Street
Barnsley
South Yorkshire S70 2AS

ISBN 978 1 47384 373 8

A CIP record for this book is available from the British Library

Printed and bound in England
by CPI Group (UK) Ltd, Croydon, CR0 4YY

Typeset in Times New Roman by Chic Graphics

Pen & Sword Books Ltd incorporates the imprints of
Pen & Sword Archaeology, Atlas, Aviation, Battleground, Discovery,
Family History, History, Maritime, Military, Naval, Politics, Railways,
Select, Social History, Transport, True Crime, Claymore Press,
Frontline Books, Leo Cooper, Praetorian Press, Remember When,
Seaforth Publishing and Wharncliffe.

For a complete list of Pen and Sword titles please contact
Pen and Sword Books Limited
47 Church Street, Barnsley, South Yorkshire, S70 2AS, England
E-mail: enquiries@pen-and-sword.co.uk
Website: www.pen-and-sword.co.uk

Contents

Acknowledgements

Many years spent in Wiltshire has proved a good basis for writing this book. However, the year that I have spent researching and developing the history of *Salisbury in the Great War* has been unexpectedly enjoyable. I have made new friends and met many interesting and remarkable people. Above all, I have been overwhelmed by the encouragement and assistance that I have received. Hopefully, no one amongst these splendid folk has been omitted from the list that appears here. If so I do apologise.

With regard to technical assistance when preparing the illustrations, I am grateful for the skills applied by my son, Alexander. In addition, the project would not have been completed without the support – as always – of my dear wife, Lucinda.

Alison Crook (Bishop Wordsworth's School)
Ann Jackson
Bob Baker
Charles Lumby
Charlotte Spender (Estate Secretary: Wilton Estate)
Chris Southon
Claire Skinner (Wiltshire and Swindon History Centre)
Clare Russell (Marlborough College Archives)
David du Croz
Sir Edward Hulse Bt
Ethel Towl
Geoff Procter
Gladys and John Waters
Graham Fry (Salisbury City Council)
Helen Taylor (Wiltshire and Swindon History Centre)

Irene Collins

Jim Fuller

Joyce Paesen (Salisbury Museum)

Joy Rutter (Wiltshire and Swindon History Centre)

Kathryn Albany-Ward

Ken and Elizabeth Jones

Kim Chittick (Salisbury Museum)

Mark Romain

Martin McIntyre

Melanie Coussens (English Heritage)

Michael Maidment

Mike Marshman (Wiltshire and Swindon History Centre)

Nick Stiven (Chafyn Grove)

Norman Thorne

Patricia and Roger Cook

Peter Daniels

Peter Smith (Salisbury Cathedral School)

Richard and Ruth Clarke (The Godolphin School)

Richard Broadhead

Richard Mead

Richard Nash

Roni Wilkinson and the team at Pen and Sword

Rowan Fitzpatrick (Head Housekeeper and PA to Lady Pembroke,
   Wilton House)

Ruth Newman

Steven Hobbs (Wiltshire and Swindon History Centre)

Terry S. Crawford

The Staff at Salisbury Reference Library

The Staff at the Wiltshire and Swindon History Centre

By the same author, *An English Baby Boomer – My Life and Times*

Prologue:
'The World... Was Very Brilliant'

On the Saturday morning of 28 June 1913, many of the good citizens of Salisbury would have had their heads down at the breakfast table, enjoying the reports featured in the *Salisbury and Winchester Journal*. The ladies might find instructions to '*Remedy Thinness and Improve the Figure*', of particular interest:

> '*Ladies who are thin, scraggy and angular, and lacking in the full rounded development which adds so much to any woman's charm, may accomplish wonders in the way of putting on flesh, filling up hollow cheeks, necks and shoulders and generally developing the figure by giving a little attention to the nervous system.*'

Instructions to remedy this situation followed, together with advertisements for products to cease discharge from urinary organs, kill bugs and fleas, cure gout and gravel and make your hair beautiful.

Gentlemen might prefer to turn to the numerous columns providing tips on growing fruit and vegetables, cultivating pansies and weeding window boxes. They might also be attracted to Lipton's advertisement for Margarine Overweight – '*nutritious as butter*', made with nuts and cream at 1s (shilling) per pound with 3lbs of granulated sugar thrown in for 2d (pence). This – to my mind – strange product – was somehow linked to encourage enjoyment of the summer holidays '*with comfort and economy*'.

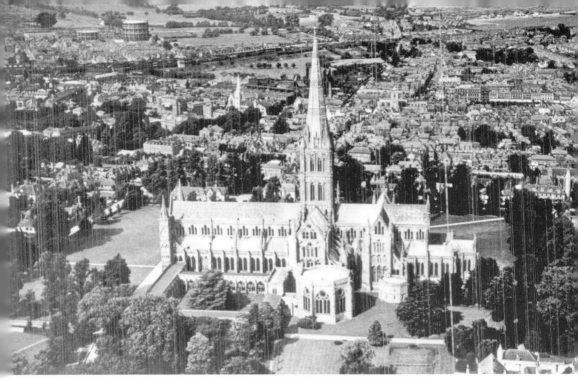

Salisbury Cathedral and the city in the early twentieth century. (T.S. Crawford)

A fashionable wedding at St Thomas's Church would shortly take place between W.J.L. Lake and Charlotte Marlow of Milford Hall. Another article that would have attracted interest was the report of the Salisbury Amateur Operatic Society's meeting where a recent performance of 'The Yeomen of the Guard' was discussed and proposals for productions at The Palace Theatre in 1914 were planned.

Results of market sales, ordinations and confirmations, local cricket matches, school sports, the weather and the Army Service Corps' sports day at Bulford Camp, some ten miles away on Salisbury Plain, would not have gone unnoticed. Life in the city and in the villages on the nearby Plain were intricately connected and would become even more so.

The bustling Wiltshire market town of Salisbury, which was established as a city in 1220, lies south of the Plain and some thirty miles north of the English Channel. It is ninety miles south-west of London and dominated by the finest spire in England that rises 404 feet above the splendid early English cathedral built in the thirteenth century and taking only thirty-eight years to complete. New Sarum, as the city is sometimes called, reflecting an earlier habitation with ancient ramparts and defences at Old Sarum, on the Amesbury road to the Plain, is watered – sometimes over-watered – by four rivers: the Nadder, the Wylie, the Ebble and the Bourne which join the Avon in the city centre. It was originally built on a plan or grid of five streets known as 'chequers' and was effectively a mediaeval 'new town'. In deference to mammon, the centre of Salisbury features the Market Square with the noble Guildhall originally constructed in 1795 and in deference to God, the Cathedral Close and Bishop's Palace with its splendid seventeenth and eighteenth century properties and luscious gardens which amble down to the river, providing excellent venues for garden parties and such occasions. The Bishop, supported by the Suffragan Bishops of Ramsbury and Sherborne, heads the diocese of Salisbury which stretches over vast tracts of Wiltshire and Dorset.

Trade provided the economic life blood of the city and the frenetic Tuesday markets generated wafts of odours from exotic ground coffee to less palatable farmyard smells that drifted through the crowded streets. All and sundry, from far and wide, gathered to buy and sell cattle, poultry and other livestock together with produce from gardens, orchards and the huge agricultural hinterland. There were also, of course, many other well-established businesses.

One such firm was James Macklin and Son, watchmakers, jewellers, silversmiths and cutlers. James Macklin was born in 1864 and eventually took over the business that his father (also James) had established at No 7 Catherine Street, in the heart of the city. In the census of 1911, when James, junior was only 47 years of age, he describes himself as a 'retired jeweller' living in the old village of Harnham (incorporated into the borough of Salisbury in 1904) with his wife, two daughters and a domestic servant. By all accounts Macklin demonstrated significant business acumen and, having succeeded to an established business which represented the old cutlery trade, for which at one time Salisbury had a considerable reputation, he retired very early in life to a beautiful home he had created at East Harnham. In 1913 James Macklin was appointed mayor of the city of Salisbury where he was destined to play a significant role over the next six years.

By contrast, another thriving business was the motor production company, Scout Motors, whose origins lay in Burden Brothers, manufacturers of church and turret clocks with a showroom in

The Tuesday weekly sale of sheep in the Market Place, Salisbury. (Peter Daniels)

The workshops at Scout Motors at the beginning of the Great War. (Peter Daniels)

Fisherton Street. At the end of the nineteenth century, inspired by their director Albert Burden, in new premises in Friary Lane, they switched to the production of combustion engines. In 1902 the clock business was sold and the company was re-constructed and re-named Dean and Burden Bros – Motor Engines, having been largely re-capitalised by the wealthy landowner and quick-witted, enthusiastic salesman, Percy Dean. In 1903 the firm commenced the manufacture of motorcycles and motorboats. It is said by Jim Watkinson in his *Scout Motors of Salisbury 1902-1921*, that the company '*may be seen as Salisbury's last real effort to remain independent in England's world of industrial endeavour.*' In 1905 the first Scout car was registered which sold for £450 (four or five times the average salary). At that time the work force had grown to seventy-five with an average weekly wage being £1 11s 3d (50 hours). By 1909 the business had grown with six cars and five commercial vehicles being built annually and by 1912 production peaked with a payroll of 150 and the production of two vehicles per week. The excellent quality of the cars, which had won prizes and competitions, attracted orders, mainly from the professional classes, from all over the country. Commercial vehicles, ambulances, buses and charabancs would continue to be produced over the coming years but events in the wider world would influence the history of the firm dramatically and tragically.

In 1908 a new industry came to Salisbury. The Hygienic Dairy Society opened a new factory just off the Devizes Road. Their remit was to supply clean fresh milk in bottles to local residents although I have seen it reported that even thirty years later milk was still being delivered by means of a hand cart, churns and a ladle, to parts of Salisbury. Nevertheless, great emphasis was attached to health issues. The churns were manufactured from a single piece of metal to avoid the joints present in conventional churns which could attract bacteria, and a feature of the establishment was the provision of bath facilities to ensure the personal cleanliness of members of staff. An innovation of the company was to install a steam whistle which sounded out over the city at 6am to signal the commencement of the first shift. In 1913 the Swiss company, Nestlé took over and expanded the facilities. Turbulent years would follow and these had their impact on the work force.

Such was Salisbury in the dreamy summer of 1913, a city where

The first two-ton Scout delivery van was sold to Hardy and Son of Catherine Street, Salisbury in 1910. (Peter Daniels)

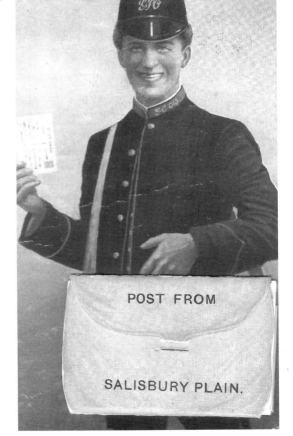

A young post boy delivering post from Salisbury Plain. (T.S. Crawford)

Salisbury High Street at the time of the Great War with the arched entrance to the Close and Cathedral spire in the distance. (Ken Jones)

you could post a letter by midnight in the certain knowledge that it would be delivered the next day, possibly even in time for breakfast; where thirty-eight species of butterflies could be found on the nearby Plain and where at least one hundred public houses were within easy striking distance of the centre of town. It will not have escaped your notice that I commenced these paragraphs by earmarking 28 June 1913 – precisely one year before a fuse was lit in the Balkan city of Sarajevo. Much has been written about this time, notably, *1913: The Year before the Storm*, by Florian Illies. Nevertheless, that year eventually rolled on.

The leader article of the *Salisbury and Winchester Journal* (the *Journal*) – which was, in fact, more Salisbury than Winchester – for 4 January 1914 commenced with these carefully chosen words:

> *'To all our readers the same old wish, which becomes not the less sincere with ripening age, "A Happy and Prosperous New Year". In spite of the boom in trade that has been slow in its effect upon an old cathedral town, most people have bidden farewell to the old year without regret and turned with brighter*

hopes to the new...With the optimism of a strong race Englishmen enter upon another cycle of days, heavily burdened it is true, but firm in the faith of their destiny, determined that 1914 shall carry the old country and the Empire a step nearer the ideal of strength their fathers set before them.'

Some months later on Empire Day (24 May), the intrepid headmistress of The Godolphin School for Girls, Miss Mary Alice Douglas, instilled a similar degree of patriotism and idealism into her young charges, encouraging courage and determination and eschewing self-pity: 'Four watchwords', she commended, 'responsibility, sympathy, self-sacrifice, duty!'

Miss Mary Alice Douglas – Headmistress of The Godolphin School 1890-1920. (The Godolphin School)

Did she know something others didn't?

'*The world on the edge of catastrophe was very brilliant*' – so wrote Winston Churchill in his book *The World Crisis* looking back on the events of 1914. And true enough, at one level at least there was little premonition of what was to come.

It was the year that Diaghilev brought Stravinsky's 'Rite of Spring' to Covent Garden and Shaw's 'Pygmalion' was premiered with Mrs Patrick Campbell as Eliza Doolittle. In the summer the season was in full swing: cricket and tennis whites, boating on the Thames at Henley, public school speech-days. The king's horse, Black Jester, favourite for the Derby, lost out to a 20-1 French outsider and the aristocratic elite basked in the warm sunshine, picnicked, partied, ate and drank. There were balls galore and the sedate waltz frequently gave way to wilder dances such as the tango, the turkey trot and the bunny hug as the young let their hair down.

All, however, was not that gorgeous. Social agitation and militant trade unionism stalked the land; strikes disrupted the economic routine of the country; the comfort of the few was being challenged by the many; the old order was under threat. And it was not just a class war but a gender one as well. The suffragette movement was also very active and in May 1914 the suffragettes were to strike at the very heart of the monarchy by attempting to breach the defences of Buckingham Palace itself, an event that resulted in the imprisonment of their leader, Mrs Pankhurst, for the eighth time.

Winston Churchill when Home Secretary in 1910. He was later blamed for the disastrous Gallipoli campaign which impacted on the lives of Salisbury residents. (Taylor Library)

Far more serious than either socialism or the suffragettes was the situation in Ireland. The programme of Liberal reforms begun nearly ten years earlier had culminated in a move for Home Rule in Ireland. Ulster would have none of it and the country was heading for civil war.

All this heightened political tension in Westminster: '*The strange calm of the European situation,*' wrote Churchill, '*contrasted with the rising fury of party conflict at home.*'

On 28 June, the heir to the Austrian Emperor Franz Joseph, Archduke Franz Ferdinand, and his wife were assassinated in Sarajevo, news that broke during the Wimbledon tournament. However, as Churchill later noted, '*the spring and summer of 1914 were marked in Europe by an exceptional tranquillity… .There had been a score of opportunities had any power wished to make war. Germany seemed to be with us, to be set on peace.*' At the end of June, Royal Naval Squadrons visited Kronstadt and Kiel and one observer remarked: 'there were races, there were banquets, there were speeches. There was sunshine: there was the Emperor.'

In Salisbury, life went on very much as usual. The leader in the *Journal*, four days after the Archduke's assassination gave the death of Mr Joseph Chamberlain who, in 1895, had become Colonial Secretary in Lord Salisbury's Conservative-Unionist Government, higher priority than the events in Europe, although it did comment with these words: '*Unreasoning anarchic folly has broken out again in a manner that makes one despair of the human race.*'

On a more cheerful note a company advertised: '*Special Offers for the Holidays – useful, light and tidy luggage*'.

'*What a magic word is HOLIDAYS*', an advertisement in the *Journal* continued on 4 July, '*It conjures up many past enjoyments and the hope of still further pleasures to come.*'

Shipping companies advertised their schedules for departure to Australia, New Zealand, South Africa and elsewhere.

Blooms of Salisbury announced: '*This sale is the LAST TIME, this year you will be able to buy Royal Worcester corsets at REDUCED PRICES. Various models at 16/11d: 12/11d; 4/11d.*'

Three days later the Reverend M.H. Knowles and Miss Agnes Rawlence of Newlands were married in St Edmund's Church before departing for their honeymoon in Wales.

On 22 July a Torchlight Display was enacted at Tidworth, on the Plain; the event took place under the patronage of General Sir Horace Smith-Dorrien, general officer commanding Southern Command, who had his headquarters in Salisbury.

On 25 July, the *Journal* reported the annual puppy show of the South and West Wilts foxhounds. The Master, Lord Stalbridge, was delighted to report a record year – sixty brace of foxes killed.

Lady Radnor (wife of the 6th Earl) wrote in her diary at Longford Castle, two miles south of Salisbury: '*The weekend of July 4th and 5th we had a large party at Longford. "Brunt" Goschew who had just come back from seeing the opening of the Kiel Canal was full of the welcome given by the German Emperor to the British Navy and the friendly atmosphere that prevailed, though everyone knew what an enormous strategic asset the canal was intended to be in the event of war. Gerald Petherick was of that party with us also.'*

On 1 August it was announced that: '*The Bishop of Salisbury requests that prayers be offered in all the churches of the Diocese on Sunday and afterwards on behalf of the peace of Europe, and suggests the use of the Collect for the fifth Sunday after Trinity, with the addition of the words "and all the nations of the world" after the word "church."*'

The Bishop's instructions had been precipitated by the declaration of war on Serbia by the Austro-Hungarians, three days previously, and the mobilisation of Russia. Germany had declared war on Russia on 31 July and proceeded to invade Luxembourg the following day.

On 3 August Lady Radnor noted in her diary that her son Ned (Edward Pleydell-Bouverie) had joined HMS *Hogue* as a midshipman, and she went on to reveal the contents of a telegram received from Captain Charles Bathurst, the MP for South Wiltshire.

Charles Bathurst entered Parliament as Member for South Wilts in 1910. (Lord Rupert Bledisloe)

'Army to be mobilised, British Fleet to protect French coasts if attacked, whole national forces available to safeguard Belgian integrity and independence.'

The lamps would soon be turned out.

The Germans declared war on France and invaded Belgium on the 3rd.

Pupils from The Godolphin, went to see a fine film at the end of the summer term – 'Sixty Years a Queen – scenes from the Crimean War and Indian Mutiny'. One pupil exclaimed, 'well, of course, it would never be like that now!'

Sometime later a member of a Wiltshire Women's Institute wrote these words:

'During the early summer we roamed far and wide over the Plain, without restriction, in search of peewit eggs and mushrooms. The cry of peewits, the lark song, the sight of the harebells, the excited jump of a hare on the short spring turf – all this encapsulated the essence of Salisbury Plain for me. In 1914 this idyllic existence stopped.'

Pupils in front of the main building at The Godolphin School in the early twentieth century. (The Godolphin School)

CHAPTER 1

1914
'Now God be Thanked...'

Although according to Foreign Secretary Sir Edward Grey the lights may have been turned out on 4 August 1914 with Britain's declaration of war on Germany, the Wiltshire community started to act with remarkable speed. Battalions of the Wiltshire Regiment were mobilised immediately and two letters were published by local Members of Parliament.

Captain W.V. Faber MP (West Hants) wrote:

'Let us in this the greatest emergency of our lives, wring the last drop of selfishness out of our hearts, and, if necessary, give up our pleasures for those in want.'

Charles Bathurst MP wrote the following words in the context of the army recruiting campaigns that were just beginning and the need to bring in the harvest from the Plain and fields that surrounded the city of Salisbury and the villages:

'May I suggest that all civilians, regardless of all social distinction, who are at present unable to serve their country in other ways should offer forthwith their patriotic assistance for the next three weeks or alternately weekends.'

It must have been obvious at the highest level that an army of 250,000, which is how things stood in the summer of 1914, would be hopelessly

The scene outside Market House Chambers at 1-3 Castle Street, Salisbury in August 1914. Part of the Recruiting Office sign – pointing to the entrance of this building – can be seen on the left edge of this archive photograph. (Peter Daniels)

Castle Street today (2015) with St Thomas Becket Church in the distance. Market House Chambers housed the offices of Francis Hodding, the Town Clerk at the time of the Great War. It is now an ASK restaurant. (NGMH)

Recruiting for Kitchener's New Army on Salisbury Plain in 1914. (Ken Jones)

inadequate to contain a German invasion of Europe. A new army needed to be formed from volunteers and Lord Kitchener, who was to visit the Plain within a few weeks of the declaration of war, set out to recruit 100,000 men. In early August he wrote to the Territorial Associations: '*It is intended to enlist as soon as possible 100,000 men and I would ask you to use your great influence and that of the Territorial Associations to secure these necessary recruits as soon as possible.*'

On 15 August the *Journal* reported as follows:

'*At a crowded and enthusiastic meeting of the men of Salisbury and district, held at the Council Chamber, Salisbury, on Wednesday evening, over 70 men announced their intention of enlisting as recruits in his Majesty's Forces in response to the stirring appeals made by Mr G. Locker-Lampson MP, who convened the meeting. The audience were roused to great enthusiasm as the men came forward and intimated their willingness to accept service in the hour of the country's need, and hearty cheers were raised when at the end of the meeting the prospective recruits formed up and marched to the recruiting headquarters, where they were sworn in and medically inspected by Dr Fison and Mr Thornton.*'

Only five volunteers failed the medical tests.

The Member of Parliament for Salisbury 'City' (Godfrey Locker-Lampson) spoke for a while, as reported in the *Journal*:

The Right Honourable Godfrey Locker-Lampson, Member of Parliament for Salisbury, at the start of the Great War. (Peter Daniels)

> *'He believed that it was absolutely necessary that we should raise in this country a second Army to support our first line, which he understood was going abroad within a very few days. He did not think it was any use trying to hide certain facts from one's mind. It was no use for them to suppose that the war was going to be a question of a very few weeks. He thought there was very little doubt whatever that it was going to be one of the severest wars this country had ever known and was going to be a war of some considerable duration. In asking for them to give their names for the purpose of Lord Kitchener's new army, he might point out that they were not being asked merely to come forward for the purpose of doing a little training, but they were really being asked to come forward prepared in all probability to go to the front and actually face the enemy in battle. (Cheers). He believed that if they did consent to enlist they would carry away with them from Salisbury the love and the gratitude and the admiration and the prayers of all those who were left behind.'*

Mr Locker-Lampson concluded with the assurance that he would watch the careers of those who had enlisted.

> *'He would do his very utmost to push their interests, not only when they were members of His Majesty's Forces, but if, after the war, they came back to Salisbury and found it momentarily rather difficult to get employment he would do his utmost to see their interests were respected. (Applause). As a small personal gift between himself and themselves he would be very delighted if they would allow him to*

give everyone who joined that night a sovereign before he went away. (Applause)'

His final words were: '*God save England and may many of you in the city of Salisbury be instrumental in saving her.' (Cheers)*

One of the first 100,000 was Private Tom Moor who joined the 2nd Battalion of the Wiltshire Regiment. Reminiscing, he wrote:

'I had worked for United Dairies 1902 to 1914 in the making of cream cheese. I started at 3/6d a week and finished at 22/6d... .Then came 1914 and the war. I can see the Wiltshires marching off to Southampton, then France, all time-serving men fit as fiddles...I still have the bob Major Stewart gave me. Fancy a bob a day and a twenty-four hour day at that. Mine was a "tanner" as I allotted my mother the rest.'

Rupert Brooke who died of septicaemia following a mosquito bite on the island of Skyros in 1915. (Taylor Library)

I am reminded of Rupert Brooke's poem:

'Now, God be thanked Who has matched us with His hour,
And caught our youth, and wakened us from sleeping,
With hand, made sure, clear eye, and sharpened power,
To turn, as swimmers into cleanness leaping....'

Momentum was gathering – this notice appeared in the local press:

'Salisbury Plain Artillery Ranges
'Notice is hereby given that firing will be carried out on the combined ranges between the hours of dawn and 3.00pm on the 18th August 1914. Lieutenant Colonel H.C.C. Uniacke Royal Artillery.'

Considering the fact that the guns in Europe would soon be heard in London, it would not surprise me if the windows and the displays in James Macklin's jewellers rattled during this barrage!

A few weeks later, this notice appeared which, in time, would be of interest to the Salisbury School and probably The Godolphin School too:

'*Public School Special Corps*
'*1200 physically fit Public School and University men to enrol as a battalion (OTC) officially authorised by the War Office for serving at home and abroad. Members defray their own expenses until the War Office takes the battalion over.*'

Salisbury and the rest of Britain was being catapulted into a war scenario that few could have foreseen although one, Major C.E.P. Stanley of the Royal Engineers, had predicted as early as 1907, how a great European war would break out and the course of the conflict. The popular *Riddle of the Sands* by Erskine Childers, which in 1903 raised the possibility of German plans to invade England, had also roused public interest, as had William Le Queux's *The Invasion of 1910* – serialised in the *Daily Mail* in 1906.

Almost immediately the *Journal* ran weekly columns (pages 6 and 7) entitled '*The War Day by Day*'.

Yes, soldiers, guns, battles, casualties and death were known to be the stuff of war however, there were going to be extraordinary consequences – well beyond Salisbury and the Plain. Far reaching implications of the events that were unfolding in the summer of 1914 would change history and could not possibly have been anticipated. One element of this change was the involvement of forces from the British Empire who brought not only change for Britain but also for those countries involved.

On 5 August the Governor General of Canada declared war on Germany. The British declaration of war had automatically brought Canada into the war because of Canada's legal status as a British Dominion. However, the Canadian government had the freedom to determine the level of the country's involvement in the war. The militia was not mobilised and instead an independent expeditionary force was raised. Prime Minister Robert Borden offered this force to assist Great Britain, an offer that was immediately accepted.

Canadians of British descent – the majority – supported this move arguing that Canadians had a duty to fight on behalf of their

Canadian Expeditionary Forces arrive on Salisbury Plain in 1914. (T.S. Crawford)

motherland. Indeed, Sir Wilfred Laurier spoke for the majority of British Canadians when he proclaimed: 'It is our duty to let Great Britain know and to let the friends and foes of Great Britain know that there is in Canada but one mind and one heart and that all Canadians are behind the mother country.'

It would not be long before Britain's other friends in Australia, New Zealand, India, South Africa and the West Indies took up the call to arms.

Now where were all these forces to be accommodated before being despatched to the theatres of war? The answer, for many, would be Salisbury Plain and many Canadians arrived just in time to assist with the harvest.

There was no room for everyone, nor was there sufficient equipment. The existing brick barracks at Bulford and Tidworth were soon overwhelmed, as were pre-war military campsites and, indeed, Salisbury itself. The peace time military district began to grow in such a manner that as the war went on, all the valleys within a ten to fifteen mile range of the city became a vast tented encampment and the Plain one huge training ground. It would become the largest military encampment in England and, in due course, this collection of individuals would threaten the domestic peace and security of the old city. As was reported in the *Sarum Chronicle* by Edith Oliver, a resident of The Cathedral Close – '*the war invisibly regulated our lives*'.

A further element of change that quickly manifested itself in Salisbury was the rapid rise of the role of women. As the men left for the training grounds on the Plain or the front, women fell in behind them to keep the home fires burning. The Women's Social and Political Union (WSPU) stopped campaigning for women's suffrage to support the war, one consideration being that support would ultimately benefit their cause, which, of course, it did.

Initially, traditional women's work was harnessed for the wellbeing of the troops in the form of Queen Mary's Needlework Guild and a branch was formed in Salisbury. The Guild was part of a national charity of ladies who raised money and supported the needy, nevertheless the war turned the focus of their activities to support the war effort. An early appeal was launched for flannel shirts, socks, sweaters, 'smokes' and other comforts 'for our fighters'.

On a wider front and in increasing numbers, more women were recruited as nurses – specifically to assist with the treatment of

Queen Mary's Needlework Sewing Party in the Guildhall, Salisbury during the Great War. (Salisbury Museum)

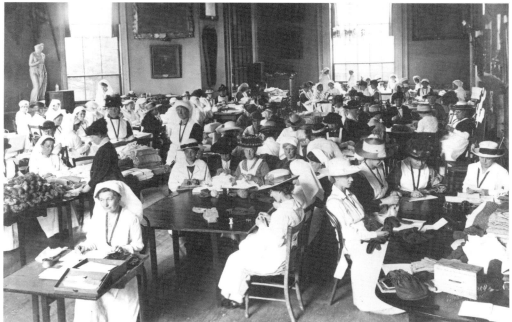

traumatised and wounded soldiers – laboured on the land, and worked in shops, offices, banks and the postal service. They also drove delivery vans for local traders, drove trams and collected fares on buses. A photograph held by Salisbury library shows a lady driver standing by the delivery van sent out by Robert Stokes: Tea Dealer and Coffee Roaster.

Cost-conscious employers, faced with the opportunity to take on women as drivers in their businesses, might have been tempted to respond to this advertisement that appeared in the local paper placed by W. Rowland and Sons of Castle Street, Salisbury: *'A Ford Motor Van will do the work of several horse vans at the cost of one. It is full 20hp speeding, reliable, capacious, quiet and the easiest vehicle in the world to manage. Canvas or steel covered – £115 – £120.'*

Women who arrived in the Salisbury neighbourhood from the industrial areas were trained in agriculture, the production of dairy produce and as 'milkers' at schools established at various locations, including Longford Castle and Wilton House. This could be a daunting experience, in many cases, when they were first confronted by cows.

A 'Milker' at The Godolphin School. (The Godolphin School)

I am not aware of any munitions factories in Salisbury, although they existed elsewhere in Wiltshire (Swindon and Melksham). These dangerous places were mainly staffed with women who worked with TNT which turned their skin yellow thus spawning the sobriquet 'canaries'. In time, the rapacious hunger for guns and munitions demanded twelve-hour shifts, frequently for two weeks at a stretch, without a break. One ex-Godolphin pupil did voluntary weekend work at the munitions factory in Erith, Kent, where shrapnel shells for naval guns were produced with the risk of hot filings jumping from the work bench on to her face and burning her. Another Godolphinite became assistant overseer at Woolwich Arsenal.

In many cases women found war work a liberating experience, providing them, for the first time in their lives, with the opportunity to earn their own money. They were, however, doubly burdened as they ran their homes, cared for their children and dealt with supplies that were becoming increasingly expensive. In addition, in the background, frequently lingered the fear of what might be happening to a father, husband, brother or son many miles away.

Some, undoubtedly tempted to spend hard-earned cash might have responded to a further advertisement placed by J. Powney of Ye Olde Corner Shoppe who was supplying *'K BOOTS FOR THE WAR – proved absolutely reliable throughout the South Africa war'*, or an advertisement placed locally by Eldridge and Young of Catherine Street might appeal:

Comforts for the Troops
Sleeping Bags
Valises and Mattresses
Toilet Holdalls
Knitted Spencers
Flannel Shirts
Sleeping helmets
Knitted Socks
Warm Underwear.

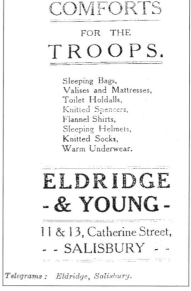

Comforts for the troops during the Great War, advertised by Eldridge and Young in the Salisbury *and* Winchester Journal. *(Richard Broadhead)*

The Council of the Salisbury Chamber of Commerce had this to say in the first weeks of August 1914: 'The Council of the Chamber of Commerce desires to make a Special Appeal to customers to pay CASH for all goods supplied to them and also to liquidate all accounts due previous to the outbreak of war. Also to place all orders with local traders.'

In the light of a major default in the world's stock markets this is, perhaps, not surprising. The London Stock Exchange was closed and remained so for months and the bank rate was raised from three per cent to eight per cent and then ten per cent within a few days.

The Salisbury and District Grocers' Association warned the public not to buy 'stocks beyond ordinary requirements' and went on to say: 'Prices of sugar have been raised by retailers owing to the fact that principal refiners have withdrawn all quotations... .Prices will be regulated each day.'

Interestingly enough, a company supplying Anglo-Bavarian Ales and Stouts were advertising in the papers at the same time, as were, C. Moody and Sons of Fisherton Street, who offered to store *'officers' baggage and furniture at moderate charges!'*

In July 1914, Royal Worcester were offering Salisbury ladies corsets at reduced prices. Dramatically, only two months later they adopted an entirely different tack in their efforts to entice the female trade to their agents, Blooms of The Canal, Salisbury.

Featuring a huge, full page, double column advertisement in the *Journal* they asked the question: *'WILL 1,000,000 WOMEN RESPOND?'* and then went on to say: *'THIS IS A WAR OF THE PEOPLE. WE ARE NOW FIGHTING for our very existence. IF WE CAN NOT FIGHT on the battlefield, we can join on the grand assault on Germany's Trade.'*

Hugely emotional in tone, the gist of the further text was to encourage British women to spend money to keep our businesses solvent and the work force viable. *'It is just pure FUNK that makes women keep their purse strings tight,'* Royal Worcester continued, and confidently anticipated that the war would end by the end of October when *'there will follow an era of prosperity for Britain such as no country has ever know before.'*

They concluded as follows:

'Will you join in the Grand Assault on Germany's Trade, and help the workers of our country by shopping NOW? If so, write us today for our new illustrated catalogue of Royal Worcester Kidfitting corsets (just published), and for the address of your nearest agent.'

As if this wasn't enough to quicken the heart and empty the purses of the good matrons of Salisbury another blast followed two weeks later assuring customers that of all the component parts of Royal Worcester's Kidfitting corsets there was *'NOTHING that is German'.* Lamb's Brewery Stores in the Market Square advertised themselves as being *'British to the Backbone'.*

Advertisement for Lamb Brewery Stores that appeared regularly during the Great War in the Salisbury and Winchester Journal. *(Richard Broadhead)*

In the certain knowledge that the war was destined to last another four years, wreak untold havoc, kill or injure millions and deliver a world turned upside down, one could read these lines and be forgiven for weeping. At the same time J. Lyons and Co Ltd sought an injunction

Lipton's the grocers at 41 Silver Street, Salisbury during the time of the Great War. (Peter Daniels)

'refraining Lipton Ltd, their agents and servants, from speaking or publishing or writing and publishing any words to the effect or of the substance that J. Lyons and Co: Ltd, or the Directorate thereof, is composed of Germans, and that by purchasing their commodities the public is assisting the enemies of Great Britain.'

At arms length from Salisbury's commercial hubbub, the social hierarchy of women in Salisbury at this time was headed by: The Dowager Countess of Pembroke (Wilton House), Lady Radnor (Longford Castle), Lady Methuen and Lady Smith-Dorrien. These good folk in true British manner, together with others, rallied support to improve the situation in which they found themselves in every way they could.

Besides support for Queen Mary's Needlework Guild, urgent assistance was required for the Salisbury Red Cross, the Infirmary and the Belgian Refugee Relief Fund. In early August 1914 Lady Radnor, whose husband was stationed on the Plain, wrote in her diary: '*Numerous meetings with Red Cross and Infirmary. Appointed Vice-Chairman of emergency Red Cross Committee.*'

On 18 August, she wrote: '*The days gradually became fuller as time went on. News of the war, bitterly anxious and we were all thankful to have work to do which kept us from thinking too much. Working closely with Lady Pembroke and Lady Methuen.*'

Early in September she appeared concerned about the flood of Belgian Refugees and wrote: '*considering what we can do in our neighbourhood*'. This concern prompted her to make rooms in the estate office at Longford Castle available for some Belgians. This must have been seen, by some, as a brave and generous act as many predominantly Anglican members of the Salisbury middle class were known to regard the Belgians – Roman Catholics – as 'peasants and artists'. However, when a priest from the local Catholic church selected two families in London, 'from the higher status of society', the problem was solved. The Count d'Alviella, an exile living in Britain, paid a courtesy visit, and met Belgian refugees in the council chamber and

Belgian Refugees – the Salmon Family – lodge west of Salisbury, at Mere, in 1915. (Peter Daniels)

an artist, James Schippers, presented one of his pictures to the City Council, following an exhibition in the Guildhall.

In contrast, an entry in the headmaster's log for George Herbert's Boys' School in nearby Wilton on 6 November 1914 reflects a different attitude: '*The sum of 4/- has been collected this last month for the Belgian Relief Fund (halfpenny collection). This collection is quite voluntary, no pressure of any kind being brought to bear. The same remark applies for the weekly intercession service for the forces held on Wednesdays at 4pm which is well attended by the boys.*'

Along with the Belgians, the Infirmary in Fisherton Street, founded in 1776 with the motto: 'The sick and needy shall not always be forgotten', attracted the devotion of the Countess of Pembroke and Lady Radnor (after whom a ward was named). From early August, when eighty beds were occupied, preparations were made to put the hospital and that of its sister, the Red Cross Hospital, on a war footing. As recorded in the weekly minutes of the management committee, plans were easily hampered. In the first few weeks of the war various sisters, nurses and the porter were called to Aldershot, the home of the British Army. The local trades people were consulted and every effort was made to economise. The nominated butcher felt unable to guarantee prices although, in due course tenders were submitted for other supplies, including tea, soap, sugar, bread, cheese, beer and fish. In early September the medical officer of Southern Command requested a costing for patient occupation and this was set at 3s 5d per day.

As the fighting on the Western Front accelerated and convoys of wounded arrived in Salisbury, the demands on the hospital increased with a '*total in the house*' rising to 121 by the end of October 1914, fifty being received on one day, which coincided with a time when fierce battles were being fought in Northern France and Belgium and where the Wiltshire Regiment sustained hundreds of casualties. '*Total in the house*' peaked at 131, one month later. More wards were opened and requests were made for support from the Red Cross and other sources to supply beds and mattresses.

Towards the end of September the Infirmary received just under £100 from the Cathedral. As the year began to draw to a close, further staff, including a house surgeon, were called to the colours, the National Institute for the Blind requested information as to how many

A typical scene in the wards at the Salisbury Infirmary during the Great War.
(T.S. Crawford)

military personnel had lost their sight and in the final week of December an outbreak of cerebrospinal meningitis required the removal of patients to the Isolation Hospital.

In November 1914 the rector of St Edmund's Church, in the heart of Salisbury, exhorted his parishioners: 'to accomplish what God gives us to do, and to endure what God calls us to bear' – adding – 'and indeed, thank God we here in Salisbury find that life goes on much as usual.'

In many ways life in Salisbury did continue as usual including ongoing health cure advertising for *Zam-Buk Cures*. The *Journal* featured a family of eleven who endorsed this strangely named medication for skin troubles, scalding, running sores and poisoned finger. *Black Cat* cigarettes were also promoted, in packs of ten, at three pence or less, depending on strength – not so healthy, perhaps, by today's standards. And a practice of dental surgeons who rejoiced in the name Shipley-Slipper of Holborn and Castle Street, Salisbury, assured patients that a complete set of artificial teeth could be supplied for 20s (£1) – adding that *'these teeth are comfortable'*. Keynes, Williams and Co were advertising spring bulbs (tulips and hyacinths) from Holland. *'Prices as long as our present supply lasts will be as*

Fisherton Street post office and cash drugs store at the time of the Great War.
(Peter Daniels)

last year', which married up nicely with the numerous pages packed with gardening tips.

The usual advertisements and notices for General Engagements, Hunting Appointments, Lettings, Property Sales, Markets, Situations Vacant, Births, Deaths, Marriages, In Memoriam, the Weather and Returning to School continued in the normal way.

The legal system also continued as routine and in August, at the City of Salisbury's Petty sessions, one, William Stirl was bound over for two months and fined the sum of one pound for stealing a chicken and some apples – value half a crown. In the Salisbury County Petty Sessions William Peck was accused of stealing a ferret and Albert Stephens was accused of desertion from the South Wales Borderers at Durrington Camp.

In November 1914, following the King George V's declaration that he would abstain from alcohol during the war and also to discourage unruly behaviour, notably by the troops and camp workers on the Plain, the County Petty Sessions issued an order closing public houses at 9pm. Ten officers and fifty men from the Canadian contingent were drafted into Salisbury to maintain order on a twenty-four hour basis. The first women police officers were introduced in due course and women patrols were introduced in Salisbury, essentially, with so many men at hand, to monitor women's behaviour and morality. Students from the Salisbury Diocesan Training College were banned from the High Street and Fisherton Street, 'as it was understood that disease had entered the city'.

Committee meetings for the local hunts, which formed an active and vigorous part of the life of the community in Salisbury's hinterland, were called from time to time as the New Forest Hunt Club stated: 'for the transaction of important business owing to the outbreak of war.'

The Tedworth Hunt met for similar reasons. Some hunts continued, however, others, such as the Courtenay Tracy Otter Hunt at Netheravon, announced its intention to abandon future meets for the duration. In November 1914 a letter signed 'PATRIOTIC' appeared as

Fisherton Street, at the time of the Great War, with the Clock Tower and County Hotel (now the King's Head Inn) in the distance. (Wiltshire and Swindon History Centre)

follows: *'Surely the thinking public when they see meets advertised in the weekly papers must truly deplore that even at this time of stress and sorrow, pleasure and luxury cannot be set aside for duty and for love of the Mother Country.'*

Nevertheless, alternative entertainment was available not far away. In mid-September management of the New Palace Theatre announced a 'Special Attraction', presenting 'The Girl on the Film', adding apologies for delaying the performance 'owing to mobilisation'. Seat prices ranged from 6d to half a crown (2s 6d). This musical farce had recently enjoyed 232 performances at the Gaiety Theatre in London and, remarkable in the circumstances, was based on the German musical comedy, 'Filmzauber', by Rudolf Bernauer and Rudolf Schanzer with music by Walter Kollo, Willy Bredschneider and Albert Sirmay. And, as if the folk of Salisbury had not enough to worry about, the same establishment followed through in December with 'The Loss of the *Titanic*', described as 'The Immortal Tale of Simple Heroism in 8 Tableaux – every endeavour is made to convey a true pictorial idea of the whole history of the disaster.' The performance also featured J.W. Warner – 'the last word in ventriloquism', adding a further temptation to attend – 'nothing so clever yet seen in Salisbury. See the crying figure.'

Public gatherings in connection with the war were also arranged. In November a public meeting in County Hall, in the presence of 'top brass', was entitled: 'The War How It Affects Us!'. 'All men of military age are especially asked to attend, and to rally to the support of King and Country in this great national emergency.'

In November J.A.R. Marriott MA gave a lecture in the Victoria Hall entitled: 'The Causes of the War'.

As the year drew to a close the population at large must have become increasingly aware that Britain and its Empire were in for the long haul. Be that as it may, this would not have been the message emanating from High Command. On 9 November 1914, Captain Sir Edward Hulse, writing from the front in one of his many letters to his mother said: *'A Captain from Army Headquarters told me yesterday that French and Joffre are eminently satisfied and extremely optimistic with regard to the situation in general. They incline to an early termination of the war; I can't see it myself.'*

Dug in, as they were, in trenches that ran 400 miles from the

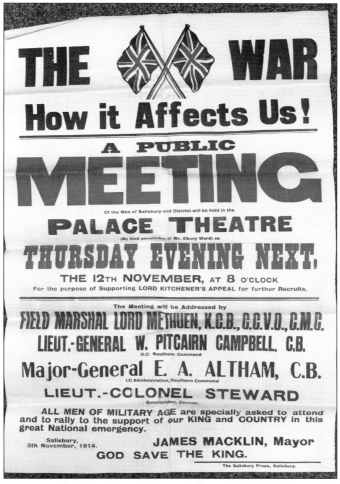

Public meeting: The War Poster How it Affects Us! (Wiltshire and Swindon History Centre)

Channel coast to Switzerland, an early termination did not seem likely. Locker-Lampson, who enlisted in the Wiltshire Yeomanry as a trooper and was subsequently commissioned, would be proven right and the copy writers for Royal Worcester's Corsets proven wrong. In fact by Christmas twenty-six soldiers with Salisbury connections, as listed in Richard Broadhead's thoroughly researched, *The Great War: Salisbury*

Soldiers, would never return and many more were wounded, missing or prisoners of war. According to Broadhead, the first Salisbury soldier to have been killed in action was Captain Walter Dawes of the 1st Battalion Wiltshire Regiment who died on 23 August during the Retreat from Mons. His address is given as Hilary House, Mill Road, Salisbury.

Although regular casualty lists began to appear in the local press, those with significant social status tended to receive special mention. One such fatality was Lieutenant Edmund Antrobus, son and heir of Sir Edmund Antrobus Bt. of Amesbury, who was killed at the First Battle of Ypres and has no known grave. The lieutenant's name is listed on the Menin Gate. His father, who had recently sold land upon which Stonehenge is sited to Mr C.H. Chubb for £6,600, died a few months later, having, it was said, never recovered from his loss.

Also killed in action in the first weeks of the war was Lieutenant Percy Wyndham of Clouds, a beautiful house just west of Salisbury. His mother was Countess Grosvenor and he had been aide-de-camp to a senior officer of the Southern Command. Also, widely reported, was the sinking of HMS *Hogue* in the North Sea. '*Extreme anxiety*', noted Lady Radnor when she received this news of the ship in which her son, Edward, was serving. Fortunately, he was rescued and returned to Longford Castle in a matter of days.

The coming of Christmas, of course, brought its own attractions and social opportunities. For Lord and Lady Radnor the year's end was sealed by their daughter Jeanne's marriage to Gerald Petherick in Salisbury Cathedral on 21 December. No formal invitations were sent because of the war but, perhaps surprisingly, German music featured in the service – 'Lohengrin' and the Lutheran hymn 'Now thank we all our God *(Nun danket Alle Gott)*. Well, after all, it would only be a matter of days before the troops were playing football, exchanging cigars and singing carols with the enemy on the Western Front.

CHAPTER 2

1915
Entrenched

The year 1914 had ended with a flourish of advertisements featuring those who had been awarded the Victoria Cross. '*There is room for your name on this Roll of Honour – these heroes would never have won the VC by staying away from the recruitment office,*' potential recruits were informed. And, as if this was not enough to prick the conscience of any malingerer the advertisements ran on:

> '*Ask your employer to keep your position open for you. Tell him that you are going to the help of the Empire.*
>
> *A Question for employers: Have you anyone in your employ who ought to enlist?*'

To date, no Salisbury soldier had received the highest accolade, For Valour, but that day would come.

On 1 January, a single-column half-page in the *Journal*, which maintained a supportive policy towards the war effort, announced:

> '*The Great Resolution for the New Year.*
> *I will be a MAN and enlist today. At any post office you can maintain the address of the nearest recruiting office.*
> *GOD SAVE THE KING.*'

Thus, the New Year opened with a realisation that a national course had been set from which there was no going back and this had been fuelled by the growing list of casualties. Five months into the war the cathedral city of Salisbury was being shaken to the core and becoming a very different place. The hair raising stories of atrocities – some real, some possibly fabricated – perpetrated by the enemy and the very real fear of defeat must have burned deeply into the psyche of the population.

However, on the home front, an immediate calamity threatened. In early January the city was subject to disastrous floods. Following the death of a Canadian soldier, drowned at Amesbury, this is how it was reported by the *Journal* in what is, in my view, charming English:

> *'Salisbury and South Wilts have this week suffered a severe visitation by flood involving the loss of at least one life – acute distress to many inhabitants, great dislocation of trade and immense damage to property. It is many years since this part of the country has undergone such an extraordinary experience, which originated in the abnormal downpour of rain in the concluding weeks of last year.'*

An alternative form of transport during the floods in, Salisbury: February 1915. (Wiltshire and Swindon History Centre)

Soldiers battling with the floods at Shrewton in 1915. (Ken Jones)

The report continues with details of the levels to which the rivers Avon and Nadder rose and *'the inundation of Salisbury Cathedral and Close, the conversion of main streets into temporary canals and the hardships and inconvenience upon hundreds of occupiers… .'* Unfortunately records do not exist for Scout Motors and I have wondered about Style and Gerrish, the agents for Axminster Carpets – flooding in their showroom could have been very damaging. Unearthing records for other businesses in the city has proved problematic so I am unable to ascertain the level of damage incurred although there is a photograph in Salisbury library of Nelson and Parsons at 80/82 Fisherton Street under fourteen inches of water.

What is certain is that the Infirmary was seriously flooded. On 9 January the entry in the weekly minutes of the management committee read: *'Entire ground floor of Infirmary flooded, considerable inconvenience and some damage.'* With more than one hundred occupants *'in the house'*, at the time, that must have been the last thing that was needed. A further outbreak of cerebrospinal meningitis and also cases of tuberculosis only added to their problems. The entry for 27 February where matron regrets that she has dismissed probationer Musgrove, makes interesting reading – *'she having in-discretely promised to marry a soldier patient after only a month's acquaintance'.*

In due course, the waters subsided and the people of Salisbury braced themselves for the ongoing situation. There would be no more singing and other larks with the Germans on the front. Reports of such episodes had recently been reported.

In an early February edition of the *Journal*, the editor wrote as follows:

> *'It was six months on Thursday since the declaration of war. That period has been the most blood boltered in the history of the world. Not only has the sacrifice of life within so short a time been unexampled but the record, though rendered for ever memorable by acts of heroism, courage and endurance is stained by deeds of cruelty, and barbarous savageness which it was believed impossible the civilised world would ever again be called upon to witness and endure... .*
>
> *'The only way to bring the war to an effective end and to secure lasting peace is to defeat the enemy in the field.'*

In the meantime the trading life of the city and surrounding villages had to continue. A meeting of the Salisbury and District Chamber of Commerce was held in early February and reported that business was booming and that 'the very large influx of soldiers to the neighbourhood had brought a very satisfactory amount of business to Salisbury'. The report continued in a vein of self-congratulation because this, it affirmed, had been achieved despite many businesses being short-staffed.

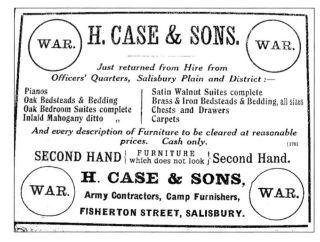

Advertisement for H. Case and Sons, army contractors and furnishers, placed in the Salisbury and Winchester Journal during the Great War. (Richard Broadhead)

However, prices were rising and at the Infirmary salaries were certainly meagre. Sisters received £30 per month, a staff nurse £14 and a probationer £8. An interesting table published in January 1915 refers to 'normal' prices compared to 'now'. I assume that the good folk of Salisbury were unaccustomed to inflation.

	Normal	**Now**
Bread	11d per gallon	1s 2d
Flour	11d per gallon	1/3d
Butter	1s 1d per pound	1s 4d to 1s 7d
Cheese	8d per pound	10d to 11d
Bacon	1s 1d per pound	1s to 1s 3d
Granulated Sugar	2d per pound	3½d

On 19 February, at the Infirmary, a cheque for 12s was issued to pay for additional telephone calls.

So one had to be careful. Self-support was encouraged on the food production front. Experts visited the area by train to provide instruction in poultry farming and one, Sanders Spencer encouraged the rearing of pigs. 'So long as the war lasts and the conditions remain at present it is advisable to make as much pork as possible in the shortest possible time. It is more than doubtful if pig breeders and feeders are likely to experience so prosperous a time after peace has been declared,' he proclaimed.

Further economy was counselled as declared in the *Journal*:

'The Salisbury Gas, Light and Coke Company greatly regret that, on account of the absolute impossibility of obtaining anything approaching adequate supplies of coal delivered at Salisbury, they must ask their customers to exercise every possible economy in consumption of gas until further notice.'

This led to a reduction in street lighting and a requirement for the police to provide hurricane lamps. Salisbury railway station's lighting was curtailed under the Defence of the Realm Act and, following rumours of possible Zeppelin raids, several warning hooters were installed in the city. On one occasion all lights were extinguished after reports of

Canadian Artillery riding past Stonehenge during the Great War. (T.S. Crawford)

a sighting over Southampton. The City Council discussed the question of insuring the council chamber against possible air attacks and the dean and chapter of the cathedral sought the wherewithal to insure ecclesiastical property.

Salisbury Plain was, by this time heavily populated by Canadian forces – some 30,000 men were housed in tents, huts and private houses, thereby swelling the regional population of Salisbury by 150 per cent. Comfort is not the word that would readily come to mind when describing their accommodation as they sang:

> *'Why did we join the army boys?*
> *Why did we join the army?*
> *Why did we come to Salisbury Plain?*
> *We must have been jolly well barmy.'*

Our friends from across the Atlantic had been inspected by King George and Queen Mary soon after their arrival in October 1914. Their majesties had praised them for their early response to the Empire's call and they would be inspected again shortly before they left for the Front in the following February. The Canadian Contingent had not fared too well in the intervening period with deaths occurring from accidents and illness, including pneumonia and meningitis. A young bugler boy had been killed in a collision on the Salisbury/Amesbury road in January, and at least five per cent of the contingent were treated for venereal disease during their time on the Plain. However, despite some

King George V and party carry out an inspection on Salisbury Plain. (T.S. Crawford)

incidents of drunkenness in the streets of Salisbury and Amesbury and carryings on with the local girls – by both the lower ranks and the officers – the Canadians were generally popular. One enthusiastic postcard read: '*Nothing like the Canadian Contingent has arrived in England since the time of William the Conqueror...The force has its own engineers, signallers, transport corps, ammunition parks and field hospitals and there are thirty four chaplains and one hundred and four nursing sisters.*' James Macklin in his jeweller's shop, when advertising Christmas and New Year gifts, had added the rider – '*Special attention given to orders for Canada.*'

Salisbury Plain: Winnie was the camp's mascot owned by the Canadian Lieutenant Harry Colebourn. (T.S. Crawford)

When the Canadians left for the front they entrusted the Zoological Society with four, possibly five, small bears, which had been regimental mascots. Lieutenant Harry Colebourn had also brought a bear with him from Canada and she became his personal mascot, sleeping in his tent. He named his bear Winnie after Winnipeg, his home town and when Colebourn left for the front, Winnie was also assigned to the care of London Zoo. To discover what became of her and how this story ends the reader will need to wait until the end of the war.

The Canadian Contingent was soon to receive high praise for its conduct at the Second Battle of Ypres despite a devastating report that from 15 April to 3 May, 1915, 208 officers and 5,828 other ranks were reported killed, wounded or missing.

Canadians were certainly the predominant force in Wiltshire, of those coming from overseas to the aid of the mother country and the empire in 1914 and 1915. It had been planned to send Australians but reports of the likely ill-effect on health caused by camping out on the windswept winter plain, certainly after a long sea voyage, led to a reversal of that decision and the troops were diverted to Egypt and eventually Gallipoli. Considering the subsequent horrors of the Dardanelles, this does beg the question as to whether they might have fared better in Wiltshire. I have seen it reported that there had been even more enthusiasm for the war in Australia, at the outbreak in 1914, than occurred in Britain.

They certainly missed Salisbury's Palace Theatre's production of 'The Egyptian Temple of Mysteries', featuring RAMESES – the Royal Magician who had appeared before the king and queen, at the Palladium, London.

A smattering of New Zealanders were accommodated in one of the camps in 1914 and these included five All Blacks, however, when the decision was taken for their fellow antipodeans to sail to the Mediterranean, they joined them.

As spring returned to Wiltshire the papers were full of a rag-tag array of news items. Conducted strolls around the historic regions of Salisbury were still being advertised, as were the services of the shipping lines, announcing voyages to destinations of the far flung Empire. In March, a letter appeared in the *Journal* from a group of women calling for signatures to an appeal requesting the internment of enemy aliens '*especially those living within thirty miles of the coast*', and within days an item appeared announcing that one, Miss Melissina Crofton, a major's daughter, had died while out hunting after being thrown from her horse which then fell on her. Also, during March, the New Theatre was featuring 'Jack in the Beanstalk – a Grand Easter Pantomime', and at the Victoria Hall the noted author, Mr Hilaire Belloc, delivered a lecture entitled: 'The Progress and Strategy of the War'. Reserved seats started at 5s and un-reserved at 6d with reduced prices for parties of soldiers and schools. With winter memories fading, a committee was set up to report on excessive damage to the roads caused by heavy military vehicles. Remarkably enough, the Automobile Association produced a map locating such damage, so motorists had been warned. At one point, it was suggested that German prisoners of war should be employed to repair the thoroughfares. Perhaps surprisingly, this did not actually occur until much later in the war.

With motoring in mind, Salisbury library features a photograph of one Rosa Bailey, working at Scout Motors. She is operating a machine that manufactures parts for magnetic mines. The company had been commanded by the authorities to turn their attention to supporting the

A Burrell TE traction engine with workers on a road near Salisbury. This engine named 'Masterpiece', was commandeered by the War Department during the Great War. (Wiltshire and Salisbury History Centre)

war effort and later in 1915 much of their machinery was commandeered and sent to Europe for on-the-spot maintenance and manufacturing operations. Such drastic action would have a serious and debilitating effect on the life of this much respected firm. Indeed, Mr Clifford Radcliffe, the company chairman who had been involved with the business for some fifteen years, and who was not above lending a hand by working on a lathe when the need arose, died suddenly in the foundry on 16 September. His death was unexplained although suggestions were made that the Ministry's actions, precipitating huge financial loss, was too much for him to bear.

These setbacks were a great shame since Scout motor vehicles had achieved a very high standard of production as is confirmed by this letter, received a few years before the war, from Dr W.W. Ord MD of The Hall, Salisbury: '*The Scout Car which you sold me in November 1905, is still running well; in fact, I think I may say she is running better than ever…her petrol consumption is remarkably small, averaging over twenty-five miles to the gallon, and she is as quiet a runner as ever. I am thoroughly satisfied with her in every way. Yours truly.*'

As already mentioned, detailed records for Scout Motors no longer exist however, quite apart from Radcliffe's tragic death and the move to France, their skilled work force, must have been affected by the recruitment drive to serve king and empire. Perhaps some men between the ages of nineteen and forty-five, responded to this notice, posted in the *Journal*:

'*Wheelwrights Required for the Army Service Corps.*
    Must be able to re-tyre, re-felloe and re-spoke. 11/- per week all found.'

The Mechanical Transport Army Service Corps were also advertising for Motor Turners, Fitters and First Class Electricians at a very competitive rate. The pressure was incessant. A further advertisement read:

'*To every good motor driver – YOU ARE WANTED AT ONCE by your King. To drive the motor transport of his new armies. Horse transport drivers also wanted age 40 – 45.*'

The all-male work force at Scout Motors at the beginning of the Great War.
Many of these men would soon be serving the Colours. How many survived?
(Peter Daniels)

Indeed, the shortage of labour on the land and in all occupations was beginning to bite. Despite women now filling many posts, this revealing entry from the headmaster's log for St Martin's Boys' School on 11 March 1915 reads: '*The demand for boy labour shows itself in the eagerness of parents to remove their children immediately upon attaining the age of thirteen years.*'

Meanwhile, the casualties continued. On 15 February Lance Corporal Cecil Rawlings was killed in action, just east of Ypres. A much-loved elder son, his family were involved in various businesses in the city, including a furniture, carpets and flooring concern in the Market Place. Cecil had been educated at Denstone College in Staffordshire where he had been a member of the Officer Training Corps and was working at Waring and Gillow, the noted store in London's Wigmore Street, at the time of mobilisation. He immediately signed up with the 12th (County of London) Battalion, (The Rangers), but was killed six months later and is buried in Sanctuary Wood Cemetery, Belgium.

On 16 March, news reached Salisbury that Captain Sir Edward Hulse, of the 2nd Battalion Scots Guards, previously mentioned in despatches and regarded as an especially gallant officer, had been killed going to the aid of his commanding officer at the Battle of Neuve Chapelle. His father had been Conservative Member of Parliament for the city from 1886–1897 and Captain Hulse was the second grandson of Lord Burnham to have been killed in the war. The family home was, and still is, at Breamore House, near Salisbury and in November 1915, Lady Edith Hulse, Sir Edward's mother, to whom he had written weekly during his time at the front, arranged for the dedication of a marble tablet and a stained-glass window at Breamore Church which can be seen by visitors. 'Ted', as he was known, had been very close to his mother who visited him at the officer's hospital in Nantes when he was suffering from dysentery and rheumatism in September 1914. Writing to her from No. 7 Stationary Hospital, Boulogne, following 'Ted's' death, another wounded officer (Major George Paynter) wrote:

'There was no finer soldier in the battalion and his men would do anything for him.'

Shortly after Christmas 1914, a photograph appeared in the *Journal* depicting Captain Hulse, with his friend Captain Warner whose brother John had contested Salisbury in the General Election of 1910, engaged in the famous Christmas truce on the Western Front. They had met Germans, sung carols and *Auld Lang Syne* together, exchanged gifts in no man's land and arranged for the burial of dead soldiers who were lying in no man's land between the opposing trenches.

Memorial to Captain Sir Edward Hulse, erected by his mother, the Hon Lady Hulse, following his death at the battle of Neuve Chapelle on 12 March 1915. (NGMH)

*Memorial window to Captain
Sir Edward Hulse in St Mary's
Church, Breamore. (NGMH)*

*Captain Sir Edward
Hulse and Captain E.
Warner in the trenches
on Christmas Day
1914. (Sir Edward
Hulse)*

'Ted's' letters that were privately printed in 1916 are a unique record of his time at the front. To re-produce large tracts of his writing, which describe the comings and goings between the enemy trenches over a number of days, would be inappropriate in this book, nevertheless these paragraphs are of interest:

28/12/14
'My Dearest Mother
Just returned to billets again, after the most extraordinary Christmas in the trenches you could possibly imagine. Words fail me completely in trying to describe it, but here goes! [Page 56]
*   The little fellow I was talking to, was an under-sized, pasty faced student type, talked four languages well, and had a business in England, so I mistrusted him at once. I asked them what orders they had from their officers as to coming over to us, and they said none… . They protested that they had no feeling of enmity towards us, but that everything lay with their authorities, and that being soldiers they had to obey. I believed that they were speaking the truth when they said this, and that they never wished to fire a shot again.' [Page 57]*
*   Meanwhile Scots and Huns were fraternizing in the most genuine possible manner. Every sort of souvenir was exchanged, addresses given and received, photos of families shown, etc. One of our fellows offered a German a cigarette: the German said, "Virginian?" Our fellow said, "Aye, straight cut": the German said, "No thanks, I only smoke Turkish"! It gave us all a good laugh.' [Page 58]*
*   'The trenches are so close at this point, that of course each side had to be far stricter. Well, he found an extremely pleasant and superior stamp of German officer, who arranged to bring all our dead to the half-way line. We took them over there, and buried 29 exactly half-way between the two lines.' [Page 61]*

And what did they have for Christmas dinner?

'We had steak, mashed potatoes, plum-pudding, ginger biscuits, chocolate (hot), whisky and water, and finished by drinking your health and all at home in best Russian Kümmel.' [Page 60]

As the grip of the war intensified the *Journal* brought forward '*The War Day by Day*' to pages two and three. The paper continued to remain up-beat with one heading announcing, ANOTHER IMPORTANT BRITISH ADVANCE, in bold lettering although a sub-section below continued, '*the nibbling process of the allies on the Western front goes on apace.*'

Sheila Dimsey wrote the following piece which can be found in *The Godolphin School 1726–1926*, edited by M.A. Douglas and C.R. Ash. Miss Dimsey was a pupil at this renowned girl's school from 1915-1919.

'The war came nearest to most of us in those lists of relations and friends on active service which were read at school prayers. Life and death stood suddenly close at hand, making us grow up before our time, and giving us unwanted responsibility, even in our own little daily doings.'

These lists of relations and friends on active service were also published regularly in the *The Godolphin School Magazine*. A typical example is that of the Summer Term edition of 1915 when the names of seventy soldiers, six sailors, nineteen doctors, nurses and others were drawn up. The Roll of Honour also listed twelve names. As the war progressed the editors adopted the practice of providing details of the relationship between the deceased and present or past Godolphinites. A father here, an uncle or cousin there, but perhaps more frequently and poignantly – a brother.

The headmistress, Mary Douglas said, 'try to dwell on the glorious deeds, not on the acts of cruelty… .'

She also encouraged her pupils to follow the progress of the war. 'We must read the papers and follow the maps', she said. 'I have ordered *The Times* for all the Houses, so that we may read the same, and the maps have been put up at school… .'

A typical analysis of named casualties appeared in the *Journal* on May Day, 1915, was as follows:

'In the casualties reported from General Headquarters of the British Expeditionary Force are the following from the Wiltshire Regiment:

Killed: three privates.
Died: one private.
Died of wounds: one private.
Wounded: One lieutenant and five privates.
Previously reported missing, now reported died of wounds as prisoner: one private.
Previously reported missing and now reported wounded and prisoner: One lance-corporal and three privates.
Prisoners: One sergeant, four lance-corporals and thirty six privates.
Previously reported missing, now reported prisoners: Four privates.
Previously un-officially reported, now officially reported prisoner; one private.'

This list named sixty-two individuals and many more would follow over the weeks and months ahead. The effect on the Salisbury community and surrounds must have been horrendous. On 1 May 1915 news was received at 38 Rampart Road, Salisbury that Private Frederick Massey of the 1st Battalion, Wiltshire Regiment had been killed at Vormezeele, Belgium. His mother, Mrs Massey, had five sons, four of whom were serving with the colours. Frederick's brother Sidney would die of wounds in 1917. On 15 June 1915, Frederick's neighbour at 39 Rampart Road, Corporal Sidney Pitman, a whitesmith or possibly an under-gardener before he enlisted, serving with the 3rd Battalion Wiltshire Regiment, was killed at Givenchy.

A pattern was beginning to emerge which is why it has been said that only fifty-three villages in the whole country were not, in the final analysis, deeply affected by this terrible war. It is difficult to analyse all the previous occupations of those appearing in the casualty lists, however, perusing the 1911 Census it would appear that most in the Salisbury region, at that time, came from relatively humble backgrounds. I have noted jobbing gardeners, farm labourers, a builder's labourer, nurserymen, a blacksmith, a boot maker, a butcher's boy, a barman, a shoeing smith, a coach painter and some professional soldiers. Thus, it is perhaps not difficult to envisage the excitement when the original call to arms and glory came in 1914. Was not the anticipation of adventure, regular pay, scheduled meals, a roof over one's head, glamour and camaraderie preferable to a dreary life in Wiltshire? A vacuous existence, indeed, on a wet winter's day on the Plain.

The story of the Annetts family is typical: a microcosmic example of the time, the place and the people. The Annetts, a huge family, some of whom I have been fortunate enough to meet including the oldest surviving member, Gladys Waters born in 1912, were based in Winterslow, a few miles to the east of Salisbury. These Wiltshire villages were positively mediaeval a hundred years ago. Gladys's grandfather, Henry Annetts, was a woodman and smallholder and had ten children – five boys and five girls. The eldest brother, Frank, was not directly involved with the war, but three brothers, John, Edmund and Christopher, went to war and two were killed in 1915, one month apart. Edmund is buried at the cemetery at Rue du Bois, Fleurbaix but Christopher's body was never found. His name is recorded on the Memorial to the Missing at Le Touret.

At their memorial service in Winterslow, their father, Henry, overcome with grief, collapsed during the proceedings. A fifth brother, Gale, had been blinded in an accident as a teenager. I find it extraordinarily bitter-sweet to relate that, saved from the horrors of the trenches, he helped his father on the farm, worked in the family shop, married, fathered two children and finally died in 1969 aged eighty-two.

Gladys's mother, Olive, married Frederick Burton, a conductor on the trams in Southampton. She was an elder sister of Edmund and Christopher. In 1914 Frederick enlisted with the Dorset Regiment before being transferred to the 2nd Wiltshire Regiment. As the months passed, the casualty lists grew inexorably and included many men from the Salisbury area, most of them serving with the Wiltshire Regiment. In 1916 Frederick and his brother-in-law, John Annetts, survived the Somme but Frederick was killed a year later near Arras leaving his wife, Olive, and four orphan children. He lies in Bucquoy Road Cemetery, Ficheaux in Northern France. Olive cared for her children with family support until her early death from cancer. She had lost her husband and two brothers.

Such, I have no doubt, is war and the consequences of war although fate seems to work in a mysterious way. Another Wiltshire family with whom I am in touch sent six sons to the war and they all survived.

Tragically, their mother died years before her time, brought on, it was thought, by months of intense anxiety.

The eldest child (Edith) was old enough to leave home and start work; her brother (Harry) went to live with an aunt on the Burton side and the two youngest (Gladys and Dorothy) went to live with Olive's sister (Lily) in Winterslow. In due course these four children grew up and had families of their own. If Olive and Frederick had survived they might have come to know their ten grandchildren. Interestingly enough, in due course other members of the Annetts family – distant relations of those of whom I have written – ran a china and glass business from one of the oldest buildings in Salisbury – the House of John A'Port in Queen Street.

In Fisherton Street, the pressure on the Infirmary did not abate, as recorded:

'War Office writes to request twenty beds reserve for urgent cases from Fovant where four thousand troops will be concentrated. [20/3/1915]

Reply that the committee will gladly deal with any acute cases in the normal way but if twenty beds are to be kept in readiness what monetary grant will be made – also no infections and VD cases to be admitted? [3/5/1915]

Letter received by committee stating that cost per head now 4/- per day. Letter to General Bedford requesting payment of the increase.' [5/6/1915]

Very busy week – 40 major ops, 26 admissions in one day, 4 cases of appendicitis. [12/6/1915]

Report by house surgeon that hospital is very full with men sleeping on the floor because military authorities send men without questioning availability.' [26/6/1915]

On Friday, 7 May news arrived in the city from a totally unexpected quarter. The great Cunard liner RMS *Lusitania* had been attacked by two German torpedoes off the Irish coast and within ten miles of Queenstown. The *Lusitania* sank within twenty minutes of being hit. She had been carrying a total number of 1,906 passengers and crew and the number of survivors was stated to be only 772. When news reached Salisbury, extreme anxiety was suffered in the Close by the sub-dean and his wife, Canon and Mrs Wordsworth. Their son, Osmund and daughter, Ruth had been passengers. Fortunately, it was reported the following day that these young people had survived and they soon returned to Salisbury. It appeared that they had both gone down with the liner but were strong swimmers and were soon picked up. On 15 May the *Journal* reported that, *'Miss Wordsworth is still suffering from the effect of the shock and bruises.'* Sir Hugh Lane, a member of the Wilton Hunt, was not so lucky. He drowned in the disaster. The *Journal*, however, continued to advertise regularly for the shipping lines and their voyages across what were becoming increasingly perilous waters.

A postal label from the experimental research centre at Porton dated 28 September 1918. (T.S. Crawford)

Morale in Salisbury was hit badly by what was described as 'a crime against humanity', and at about this time, which coincided with the first use of mustard gas in the trenches, a senior cleric poured scorn on our enemies from the pulpit, describing the Germans as, 'a people possessed of the devil'. The Germans had first used gas at Ypres in 1915 and the British soon followed. In 1916 a centre for developing chemical weapons was set up at Porton Down, a few miles north-east of Salisbury, and this would become a major employer for the region, including Winterslow. Initially, there was little defence against gas and

A Belgian and Dutch camp construction team on Salisbury Plain during the Great War. (T.S. Crawford)

the earliest instructions were to pee in your hanky and then hold it to nose and mouth. Chemicals in the urine provided some protection.

The Church of England, as represented by the Bishop of Salisbury and senior clergy, made efforts in many directions in the early stages of the war. As new camps and lines of huts were constantly being constructed on the Plain he was anxious to support the provision of recreational facilities for the troops and even the building of churches. Bishop Ridgeway was happy to place his palace at the disposal of the Red Cross for hospital purposes, if the need arose. He was however, careful to remind his flock that the requirements of the church must go on and that meant money in the face of demands for funds in support of the war effort. The church also made it clear that they viewed the war as having been caused by man's mortal sin and that rallying to the defence of the country and the Empire was a chance for Christians to redeem themselves. 'The Spiritual Call of the War,' is an expression I have noted and 'The Teaching of Christian Patriotism in Schools,' was a topic to be addressed. At a meeting of the Salisbury Diocesan Synod in April 1915, the president moved: 'That recognising in the war, a great national discipline and a call to higher aims and ideals – social, moral and spiritual – the Synod resolves to support the Bishop… .'

Or, as Miss Mary Douglas of The Godolphin School pronounced: 'The most selfish soul alive is faced with a priceless opportunity for forgetting self.'

On the first anniversary of the declaration of war, an intercession was held in the Cathedral, followed by an evening meeting at Market House, held under the auspices of the National Patriotic Organisation. The following resolution was proposed: 'That on this anniversary of the declaration of a righteous war, this meeting of the citizens of Salisbury records its inflexible determination to continue to a victorious end the struggle in maintenance of those ideals of liberty and justice which are the common and sacred cause of the allies.'

Also, during 1915, the Rev J.C. Carlisle, addressing a meeting of the British Foreign and Bible Society, spoke of the influence of the Bible on soldiers. He assured his audience that soldiers did NOT go to the Front singing comic songs like, 'It's a long way to Tipperary'; they were much more likely to sing a hymn or say a prayer for the 'old people at home and the kiddies'. I do not know how true that was.

The dynamic Salisbury Diocesan Guild of Ringers, at their annual meeting in 1915 heard the rector of St Peter's Church in Dorchester preach with the text: 'love the brotherhood, fear God and honour the King,' before naming the 173 members of the Guild who were serving with the colours. He went on to exhort his members to continue ringing on Sundays and to remember that they – even the youngest members – were carrying out God's work and that of the church.

On a lighter note, at the Petty Sessions the Venerable Archdeacon Dundas was summoned for failing to produce his driving licence. He was fined half a crown (2s 6d) and told to keep his licence in his car at all times.

The war was at this time costing five million pounds per day.

A further pre-occupation of clergy and laity alike was the vexed question of alcohol consumption. The Diocesan Branch of the Church of England Temperance Society delivered a paper deploring the intemperance among women and emphasising the need to educate children about the dangers of intoxicating substances. King George V had renounced drink for the duration, the pubs' hours had been curtailed and, in Salisbury, organised groups patrolled the streets to enforce the law and to discourage immorality and drunken behaviour. Prohibition was discussed at Cabinet level early in 1915 and further restrictions were introduced for the sale and consumption of alcohol. Later in the year, booze was banned for soldiers in hospital and at certain institutions during Christmas parties, 'because everyone knows that the majority of inmates in workhouses, asylums and prisons are there, directly or indirectly as a result of the evils of strong drink'. It was suggested that taxes be raised on beer, much to the annoyance of Wiltshire brewers, although beer was watered down when the supplies of grain and hops became limited.

Needless to say, problems continually arose. In the Salisbury Petty Sessions, a mother was accused of misusing her husband's separation allowance (the extra allowance for the war given to the wives and children of married soldiers and to the dependants of unmarried men and widowers and also to motherless children). She had taken to drink and her children were in a poor state. They would be taken into care, possibly under the protection of the Waif's and Stray's Society. A fatal brawl was also reported between three soldiers in Salisbury in April 1915 – probably due to drunkenness.

As Edith Oliver had said, '*the war invisibly regulated our lives*,' although this was not invariably and obviously the case. Country sales of ewes, rams, sheep, cattle, and horses continued in Salisbury market and numerous Wiltshire towns but the county's annual agricultural show was cancelled. However, the Great Wilton Fair was held in the autumn of 1915 as usual. Many readers will be familiar with the tradition of these Michaelmas fairs which afforded an opportunity for employers to contract with new labourers – a practice that was graphically portrayed in the film, 'Far from the Madding Crowd', based on Thomas Hardy's novel, with Alan Bates, Julie Christie, Peter Finch and Terence Stamp (1967). On this occasion in 1915, at Wilton, vacancies on the land far exceeded supply, and a military recruiting tent sited at the fair hardly improved the employers' chances of getting their man. Indeed, farmers, suffering from labour shortage, had felt obliged to make an appeal to the War Office, saying that 'agriculture ought to be treated as a war industry', and the National Union of Farmers was reported to be viewing the calling up for service of married men, shepherds, carters and cowmen, whose technical knowledge was indispensable and could not be replaced, with grave alarm. However, in the summer of 1915 the British Farmers Red Cross Fund raised nearly £2,000 and the local branch presented two ambulances for use on the front. Each bore an inscription: The Gift of Salisbury and District: No: 1, and The Gift of Salisbury and District: No: 2.

With regard to local sport, the Salisbury Bowling Club's annual report 'afforded a good deal of pleasurable recreation' – reflecting, I surmise, the age group of those who pursued this activity. However, the Salisbury Football Club had cancelled all fixtures by the end of 1914. Curiously, women, as widely reported, began to enjoy playing the game during the war and as divulged in the records of the Red Cross Society, a field in Britford Lane was loaned by one, Dr Luckham for convalescing soldiers to play football. I have not been able to find any cricket matches reported in the *Journal* during the summer of 1915, save a couple of games played between the Chorister School and grammar schools in Shaftesbury and Wimborne, although an item in the *Salisburian*, the magazine of Salisbury School (later Chafyn Grove), reflects the times: *'It being impossible to run an Old Boys cricket match without a team, and as we are unable to go to France or the Dardanelles, it will not be possible to have a Past v Present match in July.'*

At the annual meeting of the Salisbury Cycling and Social Club a membership roll of 345 was reported, including fifty members who 'were with various forces engaged in the service of their country'. The attendees went on to agree 'that all members, serving in His Majesty's forces, should be retained as members of the club until the conclusion

Members of the Church Street Cycling Club on a day out in 1914. (Peter Daniels)

of the war'. A similar decision was made by the members of the Salisbury Golf Club and a swimming gala was held by the Salisbury Amateur Swimming Club in aid of the Red Cross.

Gardening remained an integral part of many people's lives but it had taken on a new intensity following the requirement to produce food. The *Journal* regularly supplied tips – bee keeping and the cultivation of rhubarb attracted particular attention in the summer of 1915 – as did a directive forwarded from the Board of Agriculture and Fisheries, detailing new sources of potash manures, now that supplies from Germany were no longer available.

Needless to say, the debate on foxhunting, which formed such an integral part of the social life of south Wiltshire, continued as the new season approached. A report in the *Journal* echoed the thoughts of Walter Long of the Avon Vale Hunt, who believed that the course adopted of continuing hunting was the right one. He felt that hunting provided a form of training without which the nation would have been desperately short of soldiers with the necessary skills required by the mounted regiments at the start of the war. He also believed that lessons learnt in the hunting field served soldiers well when faced with the challenges found at the front. I tend to agree with him, an opinion I voiced in my book, *An English Baby Boomer: My Life and Times* (2014). Speaking of Siegfried Sassoon who lost a brother in the Great War (Suvla Bay: 1915) and was educated at

Siegfried Sassoon (1886-1967) author of Memoirs of an Infantry Officer *and much else. (Taylor Library)*

Marlborough College, twenty-eight miles north of Salisbury – I wrote: '*After reading Sassoon's,* Memoirs of a Foxhunting Man, *I question whether he would have survived the agonies of the trenches that he later described in* Memoirs of an Artillery Officer *without his earlier experiences in the field.*'

Various other hunts continued unabated, the Wilton Hounds, the South and West Wilts Hounds, the Tedworth Hunt, Lord Portman's

Hounds and others. At a general meeting of the Tedworth, the chairman moved a vote of condolence to Lady Antrobus on the loss of her husband, Sir Edmund, the late chairman of the hunt. He also noted a strange coincidence that three chairmen: Sir Edmund, the Duke of Wellington and he himself had lost their sons on the same day – 24 October 1914 – 'doing their duty to their country.' At the annual puppy show of the Wilton Hunt, luncheon was cancelled and members were reminded of the deaths of those colleagues killed in action: Captain Hulse, Captain Boyle, Major Chetwynd-Stapleton and Lieutenant Foley. Sir Hugh Lane who drowned off the coast of Ireland was also remembered. No such meeting would fail to mention the hunt record for the previous season – twenty brace killed in sixty-four days of hunting.

Besides the casualty lists which continually appeared in the newspapers, those mentioned in despatches and brave men from the Wiltshire Regiments who had received gallantry awards, were also named. Several officers had earned the Military Cross in 1915 and members of other ranks, the Distinguished Conduct Medal. After the Battle of Loos, the 3rd Battalion of the Wiltshire Regiment was addressed by Major General H.E. Wallis who concluded with these words: 'The Wiltshires, I know, will go home with a reputation second to none.'

Every level of society was beginning to be affected by tragic loss. On 25 September Second Lieutenant John Clark, also at Loos and also the 3rd Battalion, was killed in action. His father, of Canal Road, was a magistrate in the city. In October, Captain C.G. Bond, the son of a former vicar in the diocese was killed on his first day in the trenches.

In the meantime work on the Home Front, especially at the Infirmary, kept grinding on against a background of regular bouts of scarlet fever.

In September, the Faversham Ward was re-opened to accommodate wounded soldiers from the Dardanelles and in October the house surgeon once again reported a heavy week with nineteen soldiers sent from the front, some requiring drastic surgery. A sister returned from France to take up the position of theatre sister and a tax-free legacy was received under the will of the late Rev G.R. Hadow.

The Infirmary needed to keep a constant eye on the money supply and once again went out to tender for local supplies. I wonder if they noted advice provided by a correspondent in the *Journal*, exhorting the consumption of margarine as *'wholesome, nutritious and as palatable as the best butter and it is much cheaper.'* In the meantime the Electric Light Company raised their tariff by ten per cent.

In October the chairman mentioned that a complaint had been received by some soldiers, stating that they did not get enough to eat. Dr Ord was asked to investigate each case and it was agreed that, if considered necessary, the meat ration would be raised from four ounces to six ounces. Active soldiers were expected to consume 4,000 calories per day. Another complaint was received in the autumn. Sisters claimed that their counterparts, in other civilian hospitals that also treated soldiers, received higher pay. This, again, was investigated and to their delight sisters' pay was raised. About this time several nurses who had trained at the Infirmary were accepted by Queen Alexandra's Imperial Military Nursing Service Reserve. I expect they would be destined to witness some pretty ghastly sights.

Recruitment was a continuing challenge as the casualties rose and the need to out-man the Germans became increasingly necessary. Nationwide, an average of 100,000 thousand men were still enlisting every month in the spring of 1915 but, despite the age limit being raised from 38 to 40, the flow of volunteers was drying up.

In Canada, the Prime Minister, Robert Borden had already concluded that if the war lasted, 250,000 men would be required from the Dominions alone.

In Salisbury only 200 men joined the colours in the first nine months of 1915. Even announcements, in the *Journal* such as: *'MEN WHO HAVE BEEN REJECTED for defective teeth CAN NOW BE ACCEPTED providing that they are willing to undergo DENTAL TREATMENT,'* were of little avail. Emotional blackmail was not spared either in the form of shame when children returned from school crying: 'Daddy is a coward because he has not gone to the war', and it was suggested, by whom I know not, 'that ladies ought not to kiss a man who was not prepared to enlist'.

Posters issued by the Parliamentary Recruitment Committee appeared everywhere. 'Daddy, what did YOU do in the Great War?' is perhaps the most famous, designed by children's books' designer Savile Lumley. Were white feathers, signifying cowardice, handed out in Wiltshire lanes and on the streets of Salisbury? I expect they were.

A recruiting sergeant of the 7th Battalion: Wiltshire Regiment – presumably trying to persuade the lady that her husband should join up. The old tradition of the recruiting staff wearing a rosette on the side of the cap had recently been resurrected. c.1915. (The Rifles –Berkshire and Wiltshire Museum – Salisbury)

In July 1915 the National Registration Act was passed which was aimed at revealing the levels of employment by men between the ages of 15 and 65, in every trade. Anyone not already in the armed forces was required to register; the result being that the government learned that well over 3,000,000 men were not in uniform or involved with 'protected' occupations.

A letter received by Mr and Mrs H. Fooks of 49 Meadow Road, Salisbury from their son, Sapper L.H. Fooks, and widely circulated must have engendered mixed reactions to the call to arms:

'I am in a place writing this letter only 150 yards from the Germans, in a nice cosy little dug out with my instruments…You cannot imagine the conditions the trenches are in – liquid mud up over our knees and we have to sleep in these wet muddy clothes… the troops are very determined to wipe the Germans out.'

The Wiltshires.

An earlier letter from a soldier in D Company 1st Wiltshire Regiment would have also represented the kind of information received, in Salisbury, about conditions on the front and must have weighed heavily on the minds' of potential recruits:

> *'In answer to your letter and parcel which came to hand yesterday I must thank you very much. I must say that this leaves me, at present, in the best of health and unhurt, but we are very lucky to come through as we did. We have been through twelve days of hell upon earth, with German shells falling round us every day, and on the 27th we were practically blown out of the trenches by shrapnel, and it has reduced the regiment to a mere skeleton of its former self; nearly all the officers and also a great many of the NCOs and men are either killed, wounded or missing.'*

In the light of the deepening crisis, in which the government was torn between continuing with recruitment on a voluntary basis and introducing compulsory conscription, a compromise was introduced in the shape of the Derby Scheme. Instigated by, Edward Stanley, the 17th Earl of Derby, this scheme's official title was the Group Scheme. The general idea was that men could register their name – attestation – but only be called up when circumstances required them to be so. Married men would only be called upon to serve when the supply of single men had run dry. Men who volunteered for immediate service were accepted, subject to medical examination, while those who agreed to defer were sent home with a grey armband bearing a red crown to signal that had volunteered and were waiting for their call to the colours.

The scheme was not a great success and the debate for the pros and cons of introducing enforced conscription heightened. During the time that Lord Derby's Scheme remained in operation more than 200,000 men enlisted while more than 2,000,000 attested for future service. However thirty-eight per cent of single men and fifty-four per cent of married men failed to indicate their willingness to serve. The Member for South Wilts, Captain Charles Bathurst, asked the Under Secretary for State for War, in the House, whether steps 'were being taken to prevent unmarried men, suitable for military service, and not previously contemplating matrimony, from disqualifying themselves from service…by marrying in the next few weeks.' The Minister assured him that every case would be carefully considered.

In September 1915 the Trades Union Congress debated conscription and rejected the idea as reported in the *Journal* that '*both the resolution and the speeches at the TUC made it clear that the present opposition to compulsory national service is based upon the belief that the voluntary system provides adequately for the needs of the country… .*'

A month later a vigorous campaign to raise the level of volunteers, willing to serve the colours, was instigated. Meetings were held in Salisbury and the villages which were addressed by MPs, the Mayor of Salisbury and the General Officer Commanding Southern Command. The mayor, James Macklin, had previously addressed the people of Wiltshire in an open letter appealing urgently and specifically for recruits to volunteer for work in munitions factories. Travelling and lodging expenses would be provided when necessary.

The king issued a proclamation from Buckingham Palace:

'*TO MY PEOPLE*
The end is not in sight. More and yet more men are wanted to keep my armies in the field and through them to secure victory and lasting peace. I ask you, men of all classes, to come forward voluntarily and take your share in the fight.'

How about the women? I asked myself when I came across the king's words and, as if in answer, found a huge advertisement in the local press announcing an official proposal: 150,000 girls were required to take the place of male clerks and to work in the civil service, the banks, insurance offices, railway offices and numerous other sedentary occupations. Application should be addressed to Clark's College at Downton Road in Salisbury. '*A Special Short Correspondence Course*' would be available to fit young ladies for their new careers.

However, perhaps in the light of a dwindling enthusiasm for the war, canvassers, invited to send in possible names of volunteers, were thin on the ground. Children at the local schools were asked to play a part in recruiting efforts as this entry in the headmaster's log at St Mark's School underscores: '*By order and request of the Military Office, twelve of the first class were taken to the council chamber to*

GENERAL ADVERTISER, SATURDAY, OCTOBER 30, 1915.

5

BUCKINGHAM PALACE.

TO MY PEOPLE.

At this grave moment in the struggle between my people and a highly organised enemy who has transgressed the Laws of Nations and changed the ordinance that binds civilized Europe together, I appeal to you.

I rejoice in my Empire's effort, and I feel pride in the voluntary response from my Subjects all over the world who have sacrificed home, fortune, and life itself, in order that another may not inherit the free Empire which their ancestors and mine have built.

I ask you to make good these sacrifices.

The end is not in sight. More men and yet more are wanted to keep my Armies in the Field, and through them to secure Victory and enduring Peace.

In ancient days the darkest moment has ever produced in men of our race the sternest resolve.

I ask you, men of all classes, to come forward voluntarily and take your share in the fight.

In freely responding to my appeal, you will be giving your support to our brothers, who, for long months, have nobly upheld Britain's past traditions, and the glory of her Arms.

George R.I.

Declaration by King George V from Buckingham Palace in October 1915. Reproduced in the Salisbury and Winchester Journal. *(Richard Broadhead) work from 10am to 12 noon and from 2pm to 4pm on National Registration work in connection with recruiting.'*

It was agreed that 'the boys helping in the recruiting campaign should be registered as in attendance at school.'

However, as the end of this unhappy year came in sight men suddenly surged forward to sign up. Why should this be? It was probably because realisation was dawning that, with the demise of Lord Derby's Scheme, the end of voluntary enlistment and the introduction of conscription was imminent. Were these words ringing in their ears – 'Daddy, what did YOU do in the Great War?'

Businesses in Salisbury continued to suffer as exemplified by this notice, posted by Foreman and Sons, 'Tailors, Breeches makers and Costumiers':

'Owing to the large proportion of our staff having joined the Colours we find it impossible to arrange the usual summer holidays for those remaining. We have therefore decided, in order to provide them with a much needed rest to close our shop and workshops during the bank holiday week.'

Further notices appeared announcing that businesses would close during the dinner hour for similar reasons, although Style and Gerrish, in the Market Square, were defiant, announcing that they: *'Do NOT close their business in the middle of the day but do their best to attend to all customers.'*

The subject of money and finance was certainly topical and as the far-reaching tentacles of the war gripped almost everyone, the Chancellor of the Exchequer spoke: 'The man, be he rich or poor, is little to be envied who, at this supreme moment, fails to bring forward his savings for the security of his country.'

And he went on, 'you can still take your share in the great four and a half per cent war loan through the post office.'

The need to economise was also highly publicised. Charles Bathurst, the MP, writing in the *Daily Despatch*, lectured the nation on the subject of 'thrift'.

'We have to make up our minds, and at once, whether to waste or to win,' he wrote, before continuing.

'It is impossible to do both. It is no longer a question whether we shall have enough munitions or enough men to carry the war through to the goal of success but whether we shall have enough money. Never was there less thrift or more waste among the community as a whole in Great Britain than there is today, and never was it more to be deplored or more calculated to lead to disastrous results.'

No doubt the honourable member knew the country better than I do. However, in Wiltshire the populace was not lacking in generosity. The Recorder of Salisbury even offered to reduce his salary by one fifth, if others followed, in the cause of financial constraint – a gallant gesture that was not met with enthusiasm.

Others contributed generously to numerous charitable funds and endeavours. These ranged from the Blue Cross Fund for War Horses; the Red Cross; the Belgian Relief Fund; Queen Mary's Needlework Guild; The Soldiers' and Sailors' Families Association (Salisbury Branch); appeals to connect with prisoners of war in Germany and 'send a weekly gift of food;' the lady mayoress's appeal for 'cash for cigarettes for the troops' in conjunction with Mr W. Bingham, the High Street tobacconist, and many others.

The Prince of Wales – later King Edward VIII – in uniform. (Taylor Library)

Perhaps, not surprisingly, the most popular was The Prince of Wales's National Relief Fund. One list of contributors to this fund that appeared in the *Journal*, noted twenty-eight donors whose gifts ranged from three guineas to £1,000. His Royal Highness visited Lady Radnor at Longford, as recorded in her diary: *'he was charming but desperately shy and naïve in his expression of disappointment at not being allowed to go the Front'*.

However, as Christmas approached there was a distinct lack of *joie de vivre* as compared to the previous year. In 1915, the boys would certainly not be back. Locker-Lampson, on the eve of his departure for France, tried to cheer everyone up with a seasonal message of good will adding: 'I had hoped that this Christmas would have seen the end of the war. But, as this is not to be, I look forward confidently and joyfully to Christmas 1916, when I am convinced that we shall be re-united after these many weary months of separation.'

Christmas advertising in the *Journal* was largely centred on *'acceptable presents for men on active service'* which were composed of an array of garments to increase comfort in the trenches and to protect soldiers from Flanders mud, or practical items such as safety razors, aluminium canteens, steel mirrors and such like. There were notices announcing the Christmas services in the Cathedral and churches and a Special Pictorial and Vocal Concert in the New Theatre. Nevertheless, I have found little else usually associated with the season of goodwill. Even the mayor's Christmas Pudding Fund seems to have slipped off the agenda.

The Cloisters, Salisbury Cathedral: temporary crosses marking the graves of the fallen, taken from the battle front during the Great War. (NGMH)

However, the year would end with a flourish at the Cathedral. Lieutenant John P.M. Carpenter, the son of the Venerable Archdeacon Carpenter and his wife, married Miss Marjorie Ord, daughter of Dr and Mrs Ord of The Hall, Salisbury as recorded in the *Journal*:

> *'After the ceremony a large number of guests were received at The Hall and later in the afternoon the bride and groom left for London before Lieutenant Carpenter joined his regiment at Portsmouth.'*

I wonder what sentiments engulfed the proud parents as they waved the young couple goodbye. John had already been severely wounded in the Dardanelles campaign and Dr Ord must have witnessed some horrors in the course of his work at the Infirmary.

The Archdeacon and Mrs Carpenter would not have been oblivious to the dangers that their son would face. Lieutenant Carpenter was killed in action on 15 September 1916. He is buried at the Balls Road Cemetery, Flers, France, and his name is inscribed, in stone, on the interior wall of the Memorial Hall at Marlborough College, where he was educated. A temporary wooden cross that initially marked his grave hangs on the west wall of the cloisters in Salisbury Cathedral.

CHAPTER 3

1916
'That Long Lamentation...'

In the first edition of the *Journal* in January King George V's Christmas message was published, as also were greetings by Locker-Lampson from the trenches. The monarch ended his communication with these words:

> *'Officers and men of the navy and of the army, another year is drawing to its close as it began in toil, bloodshed and suffering and I rejoice to know that the goal to which you are striving draws nearer in sight.*
> *May God bless you and all your undertakings.'*

Oh dear! The year that would herald Jutland, the Somme and Verdun was upon the people of Salisbury and the world.

But as the winter gales swirled around the 400-foot cathedral spire and swept across the tented Plain, the local press tended to concentrate on more mundane matters and continued to bombard the good folk of south Wiltshire with advertisements for every kind of soap and health product. Blair's gout and rheumatic pills were popular and Zam-Buk continued to be a favourite as letters from the front, featured in the *Journal*, confirm.

> *'A box of Zam-Buk out here is like a loaf of bread to a starving man. Zam-Buk is so compact and keeps so well under the trying*

conditions of warfare that it is undoubtedly our best "first-aid".
I brought four boxes of Zam-Buk with me when I left England.'

The services of Private Abraham Acton VC of the 2nd Battalion, the Border Regiment, were even employed. An advertisement featuring this brave young man stated that he always carried a tin of Zam-Buk in his haversack. This was unfortunate because by the time this notice appeared, Acton, aged twenty-one, had been killed in action at Festubert, France. His body was never found.

The Zam-Buk company was founded in Leeds at the start of the twentieth century and the product, a traditional embrocation, is still available today. The name Zam-Buk is thought to be of African origin.

The City Council, at a meeting on 5 January, discussed the current measles epidemic and ten cases of both scarlet fever and diphtheria. Following on, they congratulated the Floods Prevention Committee on stalwart work, thus preventing a repeat of the previous year's disastrous flooding. On the same day, the Salisbury Burial Board met to discuss burial fees for military personnel.

Perusing the newspapers in the early weeks of 1916 one might be forgiven for forgetting that the country, and the Empire, was at war although a reminder of the conflict was struck by Messrs A. Oliver and Sons who proclaimed that they were happy to supply *'an officer's complete outfit'* for £22 10s. Business was booming and the Chamber of Commerce published a *'Who's Who?'* of their members starting with the bakers and confectioners (F. Sutton of the High Street) and ending with the undertakers, cabinet makers and upholsterers (E.J. Harrison also of the High Street). Many of the usual advertisements and notices, such as the hunting appointments, appeared: a chauffeur (ineligible), was wanted with the skill for all running repairs; good wages. A governess was required for two young children and an office boy was urgently needed in a solicitor's office in Salisbury. One notice ran thus:

'Fish, Game and Poultry: All-round MAN (ineligible) WANTED.
High class trade, good wages given.'

The term 'ineligible' had begun to creep in – describing those who were not suitable for military service – although a system of 'substitution' evolved, whereby 'ineligible' men took the place of fit young men in various trades, freeing them for military service. Meanwhile, another example of ineligibility was an advertisement placed by the Royal Engineers and Army Service Corps who required shoemakers and repairers *'between the age of 19 and 47 who are unfit for the fighting line and who are desirous of serving their country… providing that they are organically sound.'* They were invited to attend an examination at Moore Bros in Silver Street, Salisbury and *'requested to bring their own tools, if convenient'*.

Towards the end of 1915, H.E. Albany Ward, a young entrepreneur, had opened a 514-seat cinema in Fisherton Street – the Picture House, later to become the Playhouse where in 1962 I attended a performance of 'The Merchant of Venice' aged fifteen. He struggled to keep staff because of the war and feared 'call-up' himself but was exempted as this memorandum from Lieutenant General William Campbell of Southern Command records:

Hannham Edward Albany Ward, theatre owner, pioneer of the cinema in the Salisbury area and benefactor. (The Albany Ward Family)

The Albany Ward Empire! (The Albany Ward Family)

'I am strongly of opinion that, in helping to entertain the men in the various camps around Salisbury and in Salisbury itself, Mr Albany Ward is doing great work for the nation and I consider that he should be relieved from service with the Colours. He is giving every facility for his staff to enlist.'

Albany Ward was a truly remarkable man. A real cockney with West Country roots, circumstances arose whereby he was apprenticed to a carpenter in Ilfracombe, becoming fully qualified by the age of 16 (1895). Falling in with the first Englishman to show moving-pictures on screen, one Burt Acres, he became fascinated by the burgeoning film business and was with Acres when he filmed Queen Victoria near London Bridge during her Diamond Jubilee procession in 1897. Albany Ward possessed extraordinary entrepreneurial skills and being in the right place at the right time was instrumental in opening cinemas in many towns and perhaps, more importantly in this context, army camps, throughout Wessex and as far afield as Oxford where he was a neighbour of William Morris (Lord Nuffield). By 1919 he had built up a circuit of some fifty, cinemas, theatres and musical halls which he sold to Lord Beaverbrook. Frustrated by the need to patronise local printers, he also established the Salisbury Press in 1907 which became one of the largest printing works in the south. A generous man, he was noted for his benefactions to the city of Salisbury.

In early 1916 he took the opportunity to wish his customers seasonal greetings and announce 'the special engagement' of Zella Vondi & Co –' the most brilliant show in vaudeville'. The citizens of Salisbury would be treated to performances featuring Tiny Tim, the world's smallest comedian at forty-three inches and Elroy, 'the marvellous armless wonder who used his feet as deftly as ordinary people used their hands!' Did this not strike a strange resonance for city folk while those blasted by industrial warfare appeared regularly on their streets? Perhaps it provided encouragement to the maimed.

These wounded were not ignored and frequent reports appeared in the press. A group were taken to the New Forest by charabanc. They were lucky to have the opportunity as the consumption of petrol for pleasure was soon to be curtailed, although they got into trouble when their vehicle broke down, resulting in a much overdue return to the Infirmary. And one hundred wounded soldiers attended a talk in the New Theatre – 'The War in Pictures and Story' – by Dr Howard Barton who had taken a German bullet himself and his two sons had been injured.

As spring matured into summer, *'Empire Day was fittingly observed…by an impressive celebration in the Market Place in which both citizens and the scholars attending the various schools took part. A party of twenty-five wounded men from the Infirmary and Harnham Red Cross hospital viewed the ceremony from the windows and balcony of the Salisbury Club. The presence of men who have already served the Empire in so practical a way was exceedingly appropriate and one of the most pleasing features of the ceremony.'* So wrote the reporter in the *Journal*. The Union Jack was raised by Lady Hulse under the watchful eye of the mayor, James Macklin, and hymns and the national anthem were sung.

The mayor arranged regular events, including garden parties and in June 1916, thirty-five soldiers were taken from the Infirmary for their usual treat at the Palace Theatre, *'the full programme being given for their benefit, in addition to which they were supplied with cigarettes and chocolates, provided by the management.'* Other parties and fund raising events peppered the Salisbury social

Soldiers reclining on Salisbury Plain during the Great War. (T.S. Crawford)

calendar including a concert given by a blind, wounded serviceman.

At the time of the Summer Solstice soldiers and local residents attended the sunrise at Stonehenge in the presence of the Chief Druid.

News of the war had hit back with a vengeance earlier in the year when a full report of the virtual massacre of the 5th Battalion of the Wiltshire Regiment at the Anzac and Suvla Bay battles in 1915 was published. Several homes in Salisbury had received bad news following this disaster and an especially poignant notice was posted by Mrs Hinxman of Fisherton Street:

> *'Will any of the Officers, NCOs or men of the 5th Battalion Wiltshire Regiment, having seen Lt A.J. Hinxman after 5 o'clock on Tuesday morning , the 10th August, in Gallipoli, kindly communicate with Mrs Hinxman, 146 Fisherton Street, Salisbury. Lt Hinxman is reported missing since the 10th August.'*

Sadly this message was of no avail as Alfred Hinxman had been killed in action and has no known grave. His name is recorded on the Helles Memorial in Turkey as well as on the memorial in the chapel at Bishop Wordsworth's School where he had obtained a university scholarship in 1910.

British troops attacking Turkish positions at Gallipoli. (Taylor Library)

However, some good news was to come a week later. Lieutenant Bernard Macklin, the mayor's son, of the 3rd Battalion (attached to the 1st Battalion) was commanded to present himself at Buckingham Palace to be awarded the Military Cross. The citation was as follows:

> *'For conspicuous gallantry and initiative at Ploegsteert Wood on the night of December 6th/7th 1915. Previous to a surprise attack he took three men to cut wire, and finding six yards of water, in front of the wire he crawled through it alone and cut a lane through four lanes of wire, although a German listening post came within four yards of him. After watching this post for about an hour he crawled back to our lines, made his report and then returned to bring in the men he had left on watch.'*

Salisbury was, indeed, battered by conflicting news.

Although from my research of the *Journal* in the early months of 1916, there appeared to be a distinct paucity in casualty announcements. I suspect that this was to maintain morale. It was not until the spring that a detailed list appeared which was in striking contrast to the earlier years. On 27 May, seven soldiers were listed as killed in action, seven had died of wounds, one was missing and forty-six were wounded. Private E. Deubury, a former employee of the *Journal*, was amongst those named. These casualty lists had, by the nature of things, been largely made up of the lower ranks. In contrast, the regular deaths or injury of officers or socially advantaged military personnel tended to receive special mention. It was during January 1916 that the memorial to the Canadians was unveiled in the council chamber:

Dulce et Decorum Est
To the Honour of
Those brave men of the
CANADIAN EXPEDITIONARY FORCE
Who on their arrival in England
To fight for their Empire in the
GREAT EUROPEAN WAR
Were entertained and trained on
SALISBURY PLAIN
Many being the guests of the citizens
And by their gallantry at the front
Have since shown themselves to be
Worthy sons of their Mother Country.
James Macklin, Mayor
Francis Hodding, Town Clerk

The *Journal* on 16 January reports, *'not the least interesting feature of the ceremony was the presence of twenty-two veterans of the present war comprising the Surplus Baggage Unit, the only Canadians at present in Salisbury.'*

Francis Hodding, the town clerk, would lose his son from influenza compounded by pneumonia in December 1918.

I have already alluded to the discomfort suffered by soldiers on the Plain but Canadian officers – and others – were not above finding refuge, hot baths and good food in the White Hart, a splendid hotel in St John's Street, alongside the Cathedral Close, with a history that dates back to the fourteenth century. Their spirits might have been raised to know that earlier guests – it is claimed – had included, Queen Victoria and Prince Albert, Charles Dickens, Lewis Carroll, Rider Haggard, Sir John French (commander-in-chief of the British Expeditionary Force

The White Hart Hotel in St John Street: 1916. (Peter Daniels)

in 1914), Sir Henry and Lady Wood, Count von Zeppelin in 1910 and many others collectively termed the great and the good. Did perhaps future authors, Dorothy Sayers and Dennis Wheatley, pass through the imposing Georgian portals of this establishment? Sayers, whose father was headmaster of the Cathedral School, spent some unhappy school days at The Godolphin and Wheatley was trained on the Plain before receiving his commission and fighting at Cambrai and Passchendaele. It would be some years before the recorded visit of Baron von Richthofen (1907), the German air ace, would attract any attention!

This was, perhaps, at the higher level of social comfort and physical pleasure. However, there was plenty of opportunity for carnal dissipation and in my friend T.S. Crawford's splendid book *Wiltshire and the Great War* he goes into considerable detail of the shenanigans that occurred. With many thousands of fit and testosterone-endowed males on the Plain, and billeted in the city and villages, what else would one expect. I was brought up to believe that nice girls 'don't' but it would appear that I was either misinformed or there were hordes of girls who 'did', in the vicinity. As Crawford says, '*women in rural Wiltshire, often bereft of their own menfolk, were easily impressed by soldiers from other parts, many of whom contrasted favourably with village lads.*' He quotes from *The Gentlemen of the Party* by A.G.

Street who puts these words into the mouth of one of his characters: *'alf the (village) 'oomen today be hoors...there's one thing what 'ave got cheaper. An that's 'oomen. They do 'vling it at 'ee, wi out waitin' to be asked. Dirty bitches.* 'One observer blamed the women rather than the men who were motivated by *'filthy lust and filthy lucre'*.

Early in the war, female patrols were organised by the Women's Emergency Corps to monitor behaviour in the streets and places of entertainment in Salisbury. It goes without saying that the consequences of a deterioration of morality were fairly predictable. Brothels were recorded in the city, notably in George Street and Downton Road, in towns like Devizes, Tidworth and Ludgershall and even in the tiny village of Urchfont which shelters below the escarpment where the Plain meets the Vale of Pewsey. Cases of venereal disease soared, forcing the authorities to take action by issuing condoms and other assorted contraceptive materials to soldiers on leave. Further consequences followed loose behaviour and I think Crawford puts this very well:

> *'There were happy outcomes to wartime relationships, with some hundreds of women sailing to Australia (and other countries) as brides. However, many others were left behind to account to husbands, sweethearts and brothers who had returned from the war only to hear gossip about their women folk's behaviour and perhaps to find a baby whose father was now a long way from Wiltshire.'*

The poor Tommies on short leave, faced other problems too as, with the appalling state of the roads and services and without the means to rent a car if, indeed, such a thing was available, they frequently found that by the time they arrived home to one of the scattered villages on the Plain, the clock was already ticking for their return to the front. One, Edward Chant, writing in the *Journal* from Shrewton, outlined a solution: *'My suggestion is that at all the stations, might not the town or village committees have a cycle, which they could lend in such a case, to get our brave lads home quicker and easier than by walking.'* Was this approach acted upon? I do not know. Nevertheless at the time of writing Edward's niece still lives in Shrewton aged 103. More of this particular family later.

The transport service during the Great War suffered from lack of manpower as many men were serving the Colours. (Ken Jones)

Pupils attending the gardens at The Godolphin School during the Great War. (The Godolphin School)

There were young ladies – nice girls, of course – in the city who were involved in other activities, or lack of activities, as Mary Dalston, a pupil who attended The Godolphin School from 1916–1918 has recorded:

'Small but regular jobs such as mowing the grounds with the pony (Pegasus) who wore games shoes to perform the task. Working at allotments at Harnham; making hospital splints, crutches and bed tables in the carpentry shop; sewing sandbags, fodder bags and treasure bags'. The latter were known as 'Lady Smith-Dorrien bags' (after the wife of the General Officer Commanding Southern Command) and were used for sending 'goodies' to the troops. One contributor to *The Godolphin School – 1726-1926* wrote:

'At first it was wondered if all the bags were really valued and used. Such idle thoughts flew to the winds one wet and cold night when one of the house mistresses was "warned" for station duty. A convoy was expected. It was easy to see at once as the stretchers were taken from the ambulance train and laid in waiting rooms and on the platform that many in this convoy were terribly wounded and ill – too ill even to welcome cigarettes and hot milk. But there were those little bags – discoloured now and faded – precious possessions held fast which carried just those few things that meant to each man home and remembrance.'

Other activities noted were: milking, haymaking, collecting money for various charities, needlework, planting potatoes and devouring magazines that were full of news of the war. Milking was taken

Milking Test medallion presented to a pupil at The Godolphin School by Charles Bathurst MP. (two sides) (The Godolphin School)

seriously and lessons were provided under the auspices of the Wiltshire Agricultural Education Committee and noted by the Board of Agriculture. Indeed, Charles Bathurst took the matter so seriously that he circulated a letter to the employees on his estate at Lydney in Gloucestershire. He said: '*I should like to feel that my home and the home of every man in my employ upon my estate contained at least one woman or girl capable of properly milking out a cow.*' He then offered to pay for the training of '*any female member of your household in the process of milking and also give the sum of one pound to any trained female milker in your family...who is able to pass a test... .*'

And other points were made by past pupils of The Godolphin School:

> '*No school matches or half-holiday excursions – expense and difficulty of travelling.*
> *No riding – horses commandeered.*
> *No swimming – town baths converted for war purposes.*
> *No dances – Saturday evenings devoted to bag making.*'

With regard to keeping abreast with news of the war, the girls whose fathers, brothers or uncles could easily have been with the colours, may have responded to advertisements to subscribe to *War Pictures Weekly*. '*Something your children will want,*' they were informed with the further rider, '*Buy it now because it is the only real penny history of the Great War.*' Would '*18 large pages, full of pictures and complete stories of the war*' appeal to young ladies reading by torchlight under their bed clothes in the dormitories, one wonders.

A further publication was *The Gasper* whose readers were informed, employed '*very capable writers and artists, and those combine to produce a very clever paper...not run purely as a business concern but for the purposes of keeping the members of the Public Schools' Battalions in touch with their relatives and friends at home as well as with all those interested in the military activities of our Public Schools and Universities.*' *The Gasper* folded in 1916, probably because of the effect of casualties amongst the editorial staff.

The Public Schools suffered enormous losses in the Great War. Marlborough College, some thirty miles north of Salisbury, lost almost the equivalent of a whole generation (749) and Winchester College, twenty-five miles east of the city, lost a very similar number of former pupils. The fine neo-gothic chapel at Marlborough can accommodate about one thousand souls so it does not take a huge stretch of imagination, when standing in the nave, with the great golden reredos behind one, to visualise the impact the effect of dead and wounded had on the college community. What must it have been like, for a master to peruse the casualty figures and say, 'I taught him…and him…and him' – last year, or even last month? Arthur Robertson, headmaster of the Cathedral School, had a heart attack while digging up potatoes, although it was said that his condition had been brought on by grief from the loss of former pupils. John Bain, who had retired from teaching at Marlborough in 1912 was so overwhelmed by the daily lists of the names of boys that had been killed, whom he knew, that he decided to write poems in their memory. By 1919 he had written over a hundred poems. One such young man, who died of wounds, was Charles Lloyd Sanctuary MC, the son of Canon Sanctuary of Salisbury, and this is the poem he wrote:

What may give to the lads who give
Their own dear life that a world might live?
Honour and praise – how scant and small
A gift to the giver who gives his all.

How may we think on the lads who fling
Gaily away their own glad, sweet spring?
Who but must think on a heart so free
With a humble heart and a bended knee?

Giving as only the great hearts give
Giving your all that a world may live,
Wounded to death for us as you lie,
What may we give you, Lloyd Sanctuary?

I am reluctant to single out the Public Schools, as industrial slaughter swept remorselessly through the military forces from every sector of society. However, I would point those interested to Dr Anthony Seldon and David Walsh's fascinating and superbly well-researched book, *Public Schools and the Great War* which contains extensive information and reflection on this topic, far beyond the scope of my work.

Close to the cathedral, under the spread of a massive plane tree, reputed to have been planted in 1797, stands Bishop Wordsworth's School, the Church of England boys' Grammar School established only twenty-four years before the outbreak of the First World War by John Wordsworth, Bishop of Salisbury. The first headmaster was Reuben Bracher, a man of outstanding ability, who even found time to perform

The Roll of Honour commemorating former pupils at Bishop Wordsworth's School, Salisbury, who died in the Great War. A subsequent memorial can also be found in the school chapel after further research had revealed more fatalities. (NGMH)

duties as the Honorary Secretary of the Belgian Relief Fund for which he was decorated by the King of the Belgians. Sixty-two former pupils never returned from the war, to the city of their youth. This poem was published in the school magazine in 1916:

The Fallen

They are gone from the playground, are gone from the classroom
Are fled from the sports field, the chapel, the hall
With the first cry they left us to stem the grim war tide,
And laid down their lives at humanity's call.

No more shall we see them, no more hear their voices,
No more grip their hands, Death has taken its toll;
Red war had divided the clan of the Old Boys
But their spirit lives on – so the circle is whole.

                                                            C.F.E.

Following the eventual failure of Lord Derby's scheme and much debate, the Military Service Act 1916 received Royal Assent on 27 January 1916 and came in to force in March of the same year. It was the first time in British military history that conscription had been introduced. The Act specified that men from 18 to 41 years of age were liable to be called up in the service of the army unless they were married, widowed with children, serving in the Royal Navy, a minister of religion or working in one of a number of reserved occupations. A second Act in May 1916 extended liability for military service to married men which meant, in effect, that any male in the United Kingdom falling within these specified parameters was a soldier.

Men were allocated and called up by class, which was connected to the year of their birth. Class One was for those born in 1897. They were told that they would not be called up until they were 19 years old. Class Two was for those born in 1896, Class Three for those born in 1895 and so on, back to a birth date of 1875. A public proclamation was placed in prominent spots, advising the public the date on which a particular class would be called up. This was deemed to be sufficient notice, but in addition, generally, each man received an individual notice. It was the individual's responsibility to be alert to such notices and to report himself for duty. There were penalties for not reporting and for inducing or assisting a reservist to absent himself.

Men or employers who objected to an individual's call-up could apply to a local Military Service Tribunal. These bodies could grant exemption from service, usually on a conditional or temporary basis. The effect of conscription on the people of Wiltshire and the wider country was overwhelming and Military Service Tribunals laboured under appeals for exemptions.

An early appeal for an absolute exemption was made on behalf of the Tedworth Hunt who stated that their applicant was the only man they had – another member of staff had already joined the colours – and his work entailed the feeding and caring for thirty couples (hounds) which required a good deal of strength. It was stated that an older man would not be up to the task. The immediate response from the Labour representative on the tribunal was to suggest that the hounds be destroyed as the best solution. The military authorities however, were anxious to support hunting for the continuance of breeding and raising of light horse suitable for cavalry work and supported the application. A conditional exemption was granted for two months. Conditional exemptions appeared to be par for the course despite the range of options which appeared legion. The matter was discussed in the House of Lords and to quote from a speech by the Lord Bishop of Oxford, as reported in Hansard (4 May 1916):

> *'A certificate of exemption may be absolute, conditional, or temporary, as the authority by whom it is granted think best in the particular case. Also it may take the form of exemption from combatant duties only, or maybe conditional on the applicant being engaged in some work which, in the opinion of the Tribunal dealing with the case, is of national importance. There you have three, or you may say four, kinds of exemption – first, absolute exemption, which, again may be sub-divided into permanent and temporary; secondly exemption from combatant duties only; thirdly, exemption granted in view of some other occupation.'*

The south Wiltshire region was, of course, especially concerned with the status of reserved occupation (national importance) that applied to farming and the *Journal* listed relevant occupations in early February 1916. These included agricultural engine men and farm workers such as thatchers, shepherds, ploughmen, horsemen and wagoners. Farmers, market gardeners and stud attendants were also included. The newspapers were soon packed with reports from the tribunals.

The manager of a farm and dairy business was appealed for by his father, who was not able to work himself on the grounds of ill health. A conditional exemption was granted. A commercial traveller was granted a conditional exemption on the grounds of personal hardship and a clerk to the Board of Guardians, who appealed on the grounds that he should remain at his post in the national interest, following his senior clerk's recruitment by the army, was also granted an exemption. A butcher's manager, appealed for by his employer, was granted an exemption for six months and a hairdresser who appealed on financial, business and domestic grounds was also given a six month exemption after he explained that he had the assistance of an old soldier and another man who had been discharged from the French army on medical grounds.

Even the most extreme cases appeared to attract only conditional exemptions – which doubtless reflects the parlous state in which the army found itself in 1916 – as in this case reported by the *Journal*:

> '*Application was made by a bank manager for a chauffeur driving a motor-car daily between Salisbury and the camps with clerks and money for military requirements. The man was stated to have been refused twice for the army, but on a third attempt to have been accepted much to his surprise. He was practically blind in one eye, and protested that he could hardly see the officer's hand or the figures on the board.*'

And so it went on, although perhaps the more difficult cases arose from appeals by conscientious objectors whose attitude to combat ranged from quiet religious conviction to extreme bigotry. The arguments for and against involvement in military activities on religious, moral and socialistic grounds is beyond the scope of this narrative. However, the tribunals found themselves forced to adjudicate and the newspapers reported their findings.

The debate in the House of Lords entitled 'Treatment of

Conscientious Objectors' previously mentioned can be accessed on line.[1] Suffice it for me to report a couple of items that appeared in the Salisbury press.

In early 1916 a former chaplain of the Fargo Military Hospital, close to Larkhill Camp, writing from the front said:

> '*Out here we are all optimists with regard to the war…I wish some of these conscientious objectors could have been with me today in a town which is shelled every day by the Huns, and seen there a one-time beautiful edifice of Christianity, a one-time thriving town, desolate…. Really it is rather an insult to the men risking their lives out here to place them, even by implication, in a lower or more ignorant category of Christianity.*'

Another report detailed an appeal from a young market gardener's labourer from Salisbury, who refused the right of the British Government to take away his liberty. He had a conscientious objection to any form of service and said, '*I am not under the law of this country at all. My belief is that I am under the law of Christ.*'

The country and the Empire was generally considered to be in a perilous state so the conscientious objectors were playing a dangerous game. '*To what are these men liable?*' the Bishop of Oxford asked in the debate. '*Their friends are saying that they are liable to be taken to France and shot and I suppose that there is no doubt that this is the case*'. A recruiting officer was asked this question, '*supposing the man refuses to put on the uniform of the King, and goes on disobeying orders, what will happen?*' The officer replied, '*he may in the end be shot.*'

Away from such dire concerns there were lighter matters for the good folk of Salisbury to consider. As Easter approached Messrs Gibbs, Mew and Co of the Market Place were offering '*Wines of our Allies*'. These included Old Fruity Port from Portugal (2/6d per gallon), Claret from Bordeaux (1/6d per gallon), French sparkling Moselle, (4/6d per gallon) and Australian Burgundy (2/3d per quart flagon). To work up a thirst, residents of the city might respond to an advertisement placed by one of the oldest cycle depots in the city.

---

1 http://hansard.millbanksystems.com/lords/1916/may/04/treatment-of-conscientious-objectors

Gibbs Mew and Company's Darracq Dray, delivering to the White Horse public house at Quidhampton in 1915. They were early users of heavy motor trucks. (Peter Daniels)

Ernest James Longman outside his cycle depot in Fisherton Street shortly before the Great War. (Peter Daniels)

'To make the most of the opportunity Easter gives, you need a reliable, smooth running, wear proof cycle; one which allows you to ride over the ground in a tireless, effortless way, and makes the longest journey a pleasure.'

Did anyone spot the – surely unintentional – pun? I wonder. The cycle retailer must have been disappointed when the Whitsun holiday was postponed in 1916 because of 'the extent and urgency of demand for munitions of all kinds'.

'Shells made by a wife may save a husband's life' ran a popular slogan.

Being unable to roam the Wiltshire lanes, avid readers might have made time to devour *The Shell Girls* – a munitions factory romance, by T.A. Plummer, that hinted at sexual tensions in a previously male environment.

Returning to the city, one could attend The Empire Opera Company's 'Special Sacred Concert' on Good Friday or even 'The Girl from Utah', a successful musical comedy at the New Theatre. A month or so later a double bill was showing at the Palace Theatre – Charlie Chaplin in 'Chaplin Shanghied' and 'With Kitchener at the Front', and not to miss out the New Theatre staged an early summer performance of 'Uncle Tom's Cabin' with 'real negroes and a full chorus!' Something to look forward to might be the early summer tour of the King's premium thoroughbred stallion, Egret, who visited the villages on different weekdays and Salisbury on Tuesdays from April through July. However, John Fallon of nearby Winterbourne Stoke would not be dancing for joy. He was a racehorse owner and trainer who had fallen on hard times and was required to attend the office of the Official Receiver – Captain Tilney Barton – at the City Chambers in Salisbury. Despite assets exceeding liabilities he was unable to continue in business because:

1. He had fallen into the hands of money lenders.
2. He was holding bills for others and became saddled with liabilities.
3. Loss of business owing to the war.
4. Stoppage of racing.

In 1916, an Order in Council did, indeed, give power to the Ministry of Munitions 'to prohibit any race meeting if it is thought that a meeting will interfere with the work necessary for the successful prosecution of the war'.

The shadows of the war and distant troubles were never far away. In fact, perusing the local press for the war years I am amazed by how much international news was reported, something that rarely happens in regional newspapers today. A report of the execution of Sinn Fein rebels after the Easter Rising in 1916 is a good example. How did this news circulate – by different methods, I'm sure, and the following – from the *Journal* – makes interesting reading:

> 'The Press Bureau issued the following from the War Office: "Attention is called to the fact that a large number of homing pigeons are being used for naval and military purposes and many of these birds have been shot at or killed and wounded when coming to their lofts. The public are earnestly requested to exercise the greatest care to avoid repetition of such unfortunate incidents."'

On a grimmer note, suicides were reported almost weekly. Young men in the camps frequently became depressed by army life, and the prospects of what they would face in France or Gallipoli probably overwhelmed them. In April 1916, alone, there were cases of suicide by drowning, shooting and one young man cut his own throat.

The people of Salisbury also faced regular reports of aircraft accidents on the Plain that were all too often fatal. Although aviation in Wiltshire was in the doldrums during the first two years of the war, it soon became apparent that demand for trained airmen outstripped supply and the result was that huge swathes of Wiltshire, the Plain in particular, became a vast training base. In due course Training Depot Squadrons were organised to teach techniques in every aspect of aeronautical warfare including advanced flying, navigation, bombing and armed combat. It was inevitable that frequent tragedies would occur. The Royal Flying Corps became The Royal Air Force on 1 April 1918.

On 5 June 1916, Lord Horatio Kitchener was drowned in HMS *Hampshire* on his way to Russia. News arrived in Salisbury on market day and was met with a profound sense of loss.

Lord Kitchener of Khartoum who was drowned on his way to Russia in 1916. (Taylor Library)

The *Journal* reported: *'Not a few were moved to emotion by the knowledge that the brilliant administrator, the strong silent man of the government, the creator of England's New Army and the good soldier who "put duty first" had been removed by a cruel blow of fate.'* A memorial service followed in the Cathedral on 10 June.

Within three weeks, one of the greatest assaults in British military history was launched on the Somme, in northern France, resulting in some 60,000 casualties on 1 July, the first day.

'The blood-swept lands and seas of red, where angels fear to tread' – so wrote an unknown soldier.

A week later the *Journal* reported:

'In carrying through these difficult operations our troops have displayed the most magnificent courage and determination. The greatest traditions of the British Army have not only been maintained, but if possible surpassed. Indeed, it is no exaggeration to say that the past week has witnessed some of the greatest feats ever achieved by the human race. These deeds

Captured German soldiers helping to carry the wounded back to the aid post at Ginchy during the Battle of the Somme. (Taylor Library)

> *have not been achieved without heavy losses; but our casualties are light compared with those of the enemy, from whom we have taken over seven thousand five hundred prisoners and many guns.'*

The *Journal* was prone to hyperbole and this report ended with these words: *'In good heart and with confidence the Allies await the result of the gigantic struggle on the Western Front.'*

Despite all this and what we now know to have occurred on the Somme it is extraordinary to observe that only eight casualties were mentioned in that edition of the *Journal* and five of these were private notices in the deaths column. School cricket results, market sales, awards from the Royal College of Music and end-of-term school prizes, were, however, featured, including a note announcing the abandonment of the Wiltshire Music Festival for the duration. The *Journal* did, however, spare the space to report that a soldier who suffered from dumbness – caused by shell-shock – recovered when hit on the head with a ball while playing a game with colleagues. He found he could talk freely once again.

The battle raged on during the summer and in the last two weeks of August the *Journal* broke its silence and listed 31 soldiers killed in action, 10 died of wounds, 1 died of other causes, 189 wounded and 17 missing. According to Richard Broadhead in his *Salisbury Soldiers*, some fifty soldiers with links to the city died in that most ferocious battle which finally ran its course in November 1916.

On 16 September the *Journal* reported further without a word about British or Allied casualties:

> *'During the progress of this immense conflict over fifty-four thousand prisoners have been taken and two hundred and sixty guns and six hundred and forty-seven machine guns captured.*
>
> *These results in themselves constitute a remarkable victory. To them must be added the other losses sustained by the enemy. At the lowest calculation the total casualties of the Germans upon the Western Front can scarcely have been less than a quarter of a million in the last eleven weeks...these facts have no doubt been carefully kept as far as possible from the German people.'*

This was an editing skill that those at the *Journal* knew all about.

However, they did announce the showing of 'The Battle of the Somme – the most wonderful War Office official series of pictures ever presented' at the Palace Theatre.

In *Public Schools and the Great War*, Dr Anthony Seldon and David Walsh say, with regard to this film: '*It was seen by twenty million people in the first six weeks after its release, believed to be the highest proportion of the British public than any film since, and the government judged it a success in raising morale.*'

At the end of the second chapter of this narrative I reported the wedding of Lieutenant John P.M. Carpenter, the son of the Archdeacon of Salisbury. On 15 September he was killed in action on the Somme. Within a matter of days Bernard Macklin, the mayor's son, received a bar to his Military Cross, as the citation stated: '*He led his company forward with great dash, killing five of the enemy single-handed. When he was the only officer left in his company he set a fine example of coolness and courage.*'

So here we had two high-ranking citizens of the city of Salisbury. The one suffering grievous loss – and there would be more grief for the

Venerable Archdeacon before the war was over – and the mayor (who had, unusually, been re-appointed for the fourth year running) whose heart must have swelled with pride. Such is war and the pity of war.

A silver processional cross was donated to the Cathedral in memory of John Carpenter. It was consecrated on Palm Sunday in 1919 and is frequently used to this day.

Salisbury received its share of awards and decorations. One, Evelyn Gilroy, a former pupil at The Godolphin was amongst many mentioned in despatches. In her case this was for her work in the 'Acute Ward' at Le Havre clearing hospital before moving to a surgical ward on the Somme. What horrendous scenes she must have witnessed.

On 27 September Tom Edwin Adlam was awarded the Victoria Cross. His memorial in the chapel at Bishop Wordsworth's School, where he was educated, reads: '*The Victoria Cross was awarded for conspicuous bravery at Thiepval on the Somme. 27th–28th September 1916.*'

Tom Edwin Adlam VC as a soldier and as a former pupil at Bishop Wordsworth's School. (Bishop Wordsworth's School)

This was all the more remarkable since he had been severely wounded in the leg before displaying courage of the highest order. It is not hard to imagine the rapturous joy that the news of his achievement received in Salisbury and at his old school. All schools in the city were awarded a half-day holiday.

Adlam survived the war and died in 1975 at Hayling Island, aged eighty-one. His Victoria Cross is displayed in the Guildhall in Salisbury.

Also in September 1916, the Rev W.R.F. Addison, temporary chaplain to the forces and former curate of St Edmund's, Salisbury was awarded the Victoria Cross. Addison had attended Salisbury Theological College before being appointed to the curacy at St Edmund's. On the arrival of the news in Salisbury, the mayor cabled to Mr Addison as follows: '*In the name of the citizens of Salisbury, we congratulate you.*'

A flag was raised on St Edmund's Church and a peal of bells was rung. Ringers from St Thomas's provided assistance as so many of Addison's former parishioners were serving the colours.

The citation read as follows:

> '*For most conspicuous bravery. He carried a wounded man to the cover of a trench, and assisted several others to the same cover, after binding up their wounds under heavy rifle and machine-gun fire. In addition to these unaided efforts, by his splendid example and utter disregard of personal danger, he encouraged the stretcher bearers to go forward under heavy fire and collect the wounded.*'

Who were these 'wounded' – a label that has become so easy to apply? Some may have received surface injuries, were easily stitched up at a clearing station and returned to the trenches. Others – to borrow a few words from the poet Wilfred Owen – were in a dreadful condition. '*Bent double, like old beggars under sacks, knock-kneed, coughing like hags;*' if they could walk at all they '*limped on blood-shod, lame*' and were, in many cases, blind or even gassed. Others lay where they had fallen, their bodies the tortured remnants of systemised and mechanised destruction.

Those who were to be returned to England – following a '*Blighty*

A motor ambulance at Salisbury infirmary in 1916. Based on the Ford model-T chassis, the vehicle was equipped to transport four sitting and two stretchered patients, plus an attendant. The driver on this occasion was a soldier from 348 Company MT, RASC, Wilton. (Peter Daniels)

wound' – faced an arduous journey across rough roads, possibly in a hospital barge along the Somme, before facing despatch from one of the port clearing hospitals. Then, the likelihood of turbulent seas and if their destination was the Infirmary in Salisbury, more bumpy roads or rail from Southampton before arriving at the gloomiest of buildings in Fisherton Street where, if late, their final destination was reached in darkness. Rail journeys at that time could well have been in especially constructed 'ambulance trains', built in the Great Western Railway workshops at Swindon in north Wiltshire under the supervision of Frank Marillier who received the OBE and a CBE for his innovative efforts.

From *Hospital Barge* by Wilfred Owen:

One reading by that calm bank shaded eyes
To watch her lessening westward quietly
Then, as she neared the bend, her funnel screamed.
And that long lamentation made him wise
How unto Avalon, in agony,
Kings passed in the dark barge which Merlin dreamed.

Wilfred Owen. News of his death on the Western Front reached his home in Shropshire on 11 November 1918. (Taylor Library)

Every week, through every month and every year, the Management Committee of the Infirmary kept copious and clearly written notes of their Saturday meetings. The records of patients – '*total in the house*' – tended to mirror the battles being fought abroad. The average of beds occupied in 1916 was 145, peaking to 191 shortly after the commencement of the Battle of the Somme. Much of what I have already recorded re-appeared, in one form or another, as routine, although there were some unusual items. In early 1916 a request was put forward for electricity to replace gas for lighting in the operating theatres. The current lighting was considered inadequate for the performance of major operations and the gas company was raising its prices. A tender for supplying electricity was not accepted until the end of the year. The regular, annual tenders also appeared for supporting services; plumber (Pearce), painter (Rawlings), ironmonger (Lloyd), hot water engineer (Carter), bricklayer/carpenter (Williams), gas fitter (Pepperel).

Staff problems continued; nurses were difficult to procure,

presumably because of pressures to work in military hospitals, a porter left because his father wanted him to learn a trade, the cook was off for two months because of varicose veins, one doctor returned to a hospital in France and an advertisement was placed for an 'ineligible' house surgeon. Cases of illness amongst the staff also caused problems. These included tonsillitis, diphtheria, whooping cough, tetanus, spotted fever and German measles.

Caring for the patients was not the only concern for staff and in a rather touching memo (18/3/16) the matron appealed for financial help for the family of 'Gough the gardener' whose services had been much appreciated. He was sadly missed having died leaving a widow and three children.

The revelation of close attachments surfaced from time to time as in this letter from Captain Vivian Clay of the Wiltshire Regiment – writing from France: '*We have a wonderful lot of men here, and such a respectable lot. The more one gets to know them the more one admires them.*'

One of his men, writing home to Salisbury, had said, '*we have a splendid officer in Mr Clay and all the boys are very fond of him.*'

Comrades in Arms: 1st Battalion of the Wiltshire Regiment in 1916, shortly after the battles of Thiepval. (The Rifles – Berkshire and Wiltshire Museum – Salisbury)

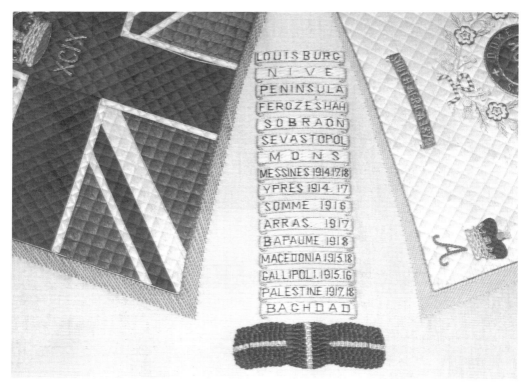

Battle Honours of the Wiltshire Regiment, worked by Richard Stagg the great-great-uncle of Richard Nash of Downton, Wiltshire. (Richard Nash)

Vivian Clay was killed on his twenty-fourth birthday on 18 October 1916. He has no known grave and is commemorated on the Thiepval Memorial on the Somme.

Another soldier, 20-year-old Second Lieutenant William Radcliffe, who had died of wounds in Gallipoli in August 1915 was remembered by a covered balcony that was presented in his memory, by his parents, as an extension to the Infirmary's Radnor Ward. It housed six beds for those requiring open-air treatment. A short dedication ceremony was held in the presence of the mayor and Mrs Macklin.

Earlier in the autumn the Infirmary records continued with a report of the visit by Field Marshal Sir John French, accompanied by General Sir Henry Sclater, and in sharp contrast the sensitive subject of venereal disease reared its head again. It was finally agreed to convert the laundry for the exclusive treatment of VD – the Skin Disease

Sir John French. Commander of the British Expeditionary Force in 1914.
(Taylor Library)

Department – and a number of mattresses were ordered from a supplier in the city – no wonder trade continued to thrive!

One contribution to the Infirmary management notes was a complaint by matron of the serious difficulty in obtaining sugar as *'local firms are being made to supply the army'.*

Indeed, as 1916 continued, the question of food supply was becoming more acute. One report stated that 'owing to various circumstances connected with the war, the supplies of sugar, available for use by the public at large, are only three-quarters of what they were in 1915'. Sugar was available for the army and for commercial traders but private families who wished to preserve their own fruit, which was actively encouraged, were directed to the use of glucose as a substitute for sugar, which was sold under the name of corn syrup. Another important source of nutrition was cheese and Charles Bathurst raised the question with the Parliamentary Secretary to the Board of Agriculture. He wanted to know whether the board was aware that the price of rennet had risen by six-fold since the beginning of the war and that this was affecting the cost of the production of cheese in Wiltshire and elsewhere. Despite folk being disinclined to keep chickens for fear of annoying the neighbours, poultry keeping was also greatly encouraged. Such troublesome neighbours, it was suggested, should be regarded as unpatriotic in the face of the national emergency.

Every effort was, of course, made to encourage efficient farming for food production and an enthusiasm for 'patriotic housekeeping' was instilled in the population at large. Earlier in the year an exhibition had been held at the City Hall in Salisbury, under the patronage of Lady Hulse. There were lectures and stalls that addressed such topics as housewifery, labour saving food production, cooking and hay-box demonstrations, 'The Pudding Lady – Miss L. Hall', and even a competition for the best set of weekly income and expenditure accounts.

In the autumn of 1916, Captain Bathurst, ever active on behalf of his constituents, asked the President of the Board of Trade how much the price of food had risen since August 1914. He was informed that the retail cost of the principal articles of food had risen by sixty-five per cent and that the general rise in cost of living was forty-five per cent.

Another autumnal problem was dealing with lighting restrictions. It should be remembered that Daylight Saving had been introduced for the first time in May 1916. The annual Salisbury fair was closed at 9pm and street lights were extinguished ninety minutes after sunset. Those herding animals were required to carry lamps, thirty minutes each side of sunset and sunrise. The Bishop of Salisbury was none too happy about the effect lighting restrictions would have on evening congregations. It was even suggested that hymns might be projected on to screens by magic lanterns before good Christian folk abandoned their evening worship. Needless to say the courts were packed with cases relating to lighting offences as well as the usual list of misdemeanours such as using a house for an unlawful purpose, assaulting a policeman, theft of a bicycle, beating horses, hawking at the camps and reckless driving.

This jingle appeared in *Punch*:

'O Matthew Arnold you were right,
We need more sweetness and more light,
For 'til we break the brutal foe
Our sugar's short, our lights are low.'

As this dismal year ended the usual flurry of Christmas gift advertising appeared in the press. Cigarettes for the troops featured significantly.

One could purchase 280 Wild Woodbines for 3s 3d and 1,000 Navy Cut for 16s. No doubt the heart of Geoffrey Studdert-Kennedy MC,

GOOD THINGS TO EAT ::
& SOMETHING TO SMOKE.

A large choice of both these may be seen in my shop, and a parcel made up of them is certain to be made VERY WELCOME IN THE TRENCHES.

Give your order early. It will be packed free of charge, and sent over to the post or rail what ever day you wish.

Telephone No. 179.

Advertisement for Robert Stokes, the tobacconist, that appeared regularly in the Salisbury and Winchester Journal *during the Great War. (Richard Broadhead)*

the famous chaplain who had volunteered to serve on the Western Front, would have glowed with pleasure. Known as 'Woodbine Willie' he relentlessly supplied ciggies to the troops, and even wrote *Rough Rhymes of a Padre*. The role of the chaplain must have been heartrending, especially at dawn when attending the execution of deserters or those charged with cowardice. As mentioned in *Public Schools and the Great War*, there were only 117 chaplains to the forces in 1914, a figure that rose to 3,475 by 1918. Studdert-Kennedy's grandson, Andrew is currently (2015) the Rural Dean of Marlborough. Nevertheless the older man had become bitter and despairing by the end of the Great War. Historian, Richard Holmes recorded his words: '*What the bloody hell is the church doing here? An amateur stretcherbearer or amateur undertaker? Was that all a Christian priest could do in the ruin of this rotten civilisation?*'

On a cheerful note the year ended with the marriage of the mayor's daughter, Dulcie to Lieutenant A. Gee-Williams and perhaps, morale boosting rather than jolly, the showing of 'His Majesty the King, with his Armies on the Somme – the new official war picture' – at Albany Ward's Picture House.

CHAPTER 4

1917

Let Them Eat Bread

Did, perhaps, the wounded officers who had returned from the godforsaken mud and gore of the Western Front to occupy the twenty-two beds of the auxiliary hospital at Longford Castle believe that they had awoken in heaven? On the walls of the splendid rooms, to which they had full access, hung a remarkable collection of old masters. Reviewed in *The Times Literary Supplement* in 1909: *'it still ranks amongst one of the most splendid of the older collections of pictures in the kingdom.'* The writer of these words was referring to *Erasmus* by Holbein, which had been brought to England with a letter of introduction to Sir Thomas Moore, *Juan de Pareja* by Velazquez, several fine paintings by Rubens and Van Dyck, seven Gainsboroughs and works by Reynolds, Claude and Murillo.

Longford Castle, the fifteenth-century seat of the Earl and Countess of Radnor and situated two miles south of Salisbury, is one of the finest houses in Wiltshire. It stands, magnificently, by the Avon in a park of some 250 acres.

During the Great War, the earl served as a colonel in the army, initially stationed on the Plain and subsequently posted to India. Lady Radnor was very active in charitable foundations, notably the Red Cross and the Salisbury Infirmary. Her name and that of her husband frequently appeared on lists of subscriptions to various good causes. Medical care and good nursing was obviously a matter of the heart for

Longford Castle: the fifteenth-century seat of the Earl and Countess of Radnor.
(The Wiltshire and Swindon History Centre)

her ladyship as this letter to the *Journal*, in her capacity as Chairman of the Wiltshire Nursing Association, indicates:

'Sir: During the last week universal attention has been called to the national importance of the preservation of infant life. It has been shown that with this object in view, much work has already been done in boroughs and urban districts by the establishment of Infant Clinics and Maternity Hospitals. In the rural districts the provision of skilled attention to women at their confinements and subsequent infant health visiting must be the work of the district nurses and midwives. The County Nursing Association has done its best for many years to train these nurses and midwives for the rural areas of the county. We have constantly lacked sufficient funds to train as many as were needed. Now to the lack of funds is added the difficulty of obtaining sufficient candidates.

The Director of Women's National Service has stated that the work of a district nurse is of as great importance to the nation as work on the land or on any other National Service. I therefore *urge women and girls to take up district nursing as their profession and come forward at once to commence training.'*

Signed '*Julian Radnor*', her ladyship invited applications to be sent to her at Longford Castle, where she had already taken informal steps to house Belgian refugees and soldiers. Unfortunately, she was not able to care for her own eldest son, Viscount Folkestone, who was soon to be languishing in a hospital in Alexandria with a gunshot wound and compound fracture of the leg.

However, in 1917 her activities were required to be placed on a formal basis and in February she received a letter from the Secretary of the Committee for the Medical History of the War enclosing a questionnaire that required completion and a statement of funding by the authorities was proposed and agreed.

Amongst relevant information supplied was a list of theatre equipment, blankets, linen, clothing, surgical appliances, furniture, wheelchairs and linoleum throughout. Although part of the house was set aside for private residence, officers were entertained as guests and the grounds which included free access to amenities such as fishing, boating and tennis were available to them. It is unlikely that the inhabitants at Longford would have taken note of a letter that appeared in the Salisbury press, during the freezing winter of 1917, signed CHILLI:

'Sir, Some of the folk who are not well-clad in the present searching weather may not know that a newspaper – or other paper – folded thickly and longwise and wrapped round the body, underneath waistcoat or blouse, will afford a good deal of comfort and protection. Sheets of paper are also useful where blankets are scarce, if placed between the layers of the bed covering.'

Indeed, the Headmaster of St Mark's school logged: '*A heavy snowstorm has caused much absence from school.*'

Lady Radnor acted as Commandant and the Medical Officer was Dr Renfoe, a leading surgeon in the area who enjoyed a reputation for being extremely able. Other staff included Matron Nicholson who, the records detail, '*was a good nurse but gave Lady Radnor trouble over*

*The presentation of an ambulance in the Market Place, Salisbury, to the 5*th *Wilts VAD by the Royal Antediluvian Order of Buffaloes (RAOB) for use by the local VAD/Red Cross hospitals c. 1917. (Salisbury Museum)*

the staff. Perhaps, too many were pretty and young and she was grey haired and not sympathetic with young things.' With an abundance of handsome officers in the castle – one can imagine!

The cook certainly had her work cut out, supplying three meals a day for the soldiers and attendant staff. This would include nurses and VADs (Voluntary Aid Detachments; some of whom had recently left The Godolphin School), kitchen staff and laundry maids amounting to more than thirty place settings for each meal.

Many VADs came from smart addresses. They were not nurses and, initially, were expected to carry out the kind of duties mother would designate to her servants at home. Some staff were paid although many gave their time without charge. Apparently one, Cornelia Wyatt-Edwards was encouraged to 'do her bit', providing she continued to double up as chauffeur for her father. In due course, first-hand experience of the pressures and horrors of the war seared nursing skills into the capabilities of these brave young ladies, dozens of whom lost their lives, were wounded or suffered from serious infections, including the Spanish influenza. In York Minster there is a memorial to the women of the British Empire who gave their lives during the Great War.

There were many VAD hospitals in Wiltshire during the Great War, some sited in small villages such as Ramsbury, Sutton Veny and Mere, while others were in the larger towns. Wilton House, the home of Lord Pembroke, was especially renowned. Extensive research not withstanding and after making contact with his lordship's personal assistant, I have been unable to unearth records, with the sole exception of a collection of drawings, anecdotes and poems housed at the Wiltshire and Swindon History Centre in Chippenham, and donated by Ann Jackson, the great-niece of the rather beautiful Sister Mabel Myring.

Wilton House: the seat of the Earl and Countess of Pembroke. (The Wiltshire and Swindon History Centre)

'But when 'settling time' was come
You think she never raised a thumb.
"How d'you feel, my child, tonight?"
She would ask you, most polite;
"Any aspirins? Any pills?"
And although she well can straff,
She can also make you laugh.'
Wilton House: Salisbury: Charles Bowman, Second Lieutenant,
11th Battalion (Pioneers), The King's (Liverpool Regiment). A
Victim.

Lord and Lady Radnor were notably generous, however, the Countess kept meticulous accounts helped by the Red Cross staff and office staff at the Infirmary. The archives held in Chippenham include volumes of detailed records of daily meals and those who attended, not to mention the extensive cellar records. Who paid for the fine wines, whiskies, brandies and champagne? It is not clear, although it would not surprise me if the Radnors footed the bill for their gallant officers. In February 1917 Lady Radnor received a letter from a government office, via Basil Hankey of the Wiltshire Branch of the British Red Cross Society, which read: '*I have to ask you to be kind enough to inform the Auxiliary Hospitals in your County that they are required to furnish an income and expenditure account and balance sheet of their hospital in view of the fact that they have been in receipt of government and public money.*'

In an age where the richest one per cent of the nation controlled some seventy per cent of the country's wealth, the financial dealings at Longford were carefully logged. Even, the market garden and the game department kept records of their supplies to the kitchen as this schedule records:

Game supplied to Castle by Game Dept.
Year ending March 31st, 1916.

275 pheasants @ 2/6d	£34 7s 6d
336 partridges @3/9d brace	£31 0s 0d
13 wild duck	
6 wood pigeons	
11 snipe	

14 woodcock
104 hares @ 2/6d   £13 0s 0d
776 rabbits @ 8d   £25 17s 4d
1 landrail
2 teal
Total: 1,538   £104 4s 10d

On receipt of the accounts, on this first occasion, Basil Hankey wrote to thank Lady Radnor adding, '*I wish all in the county were as clear as yours.*'

Despite a context of what would appear to be significant wealth, the countess's attention to detail with regard to financial matters was exemplary as this letter from her private secretary to Mr E.W. Judd, the butcher in Catherine Street, Salisbury exemplifies:

'Dear Sir
Lady Radnor desires me to call your attention to the fact that in August you charged for ribs of beef at 1/3d per pound, liver 1/2d per pound and shoulder of mutton at 1/4d. Lady Radnor has paid her other Salisbury butcher for ribs of beef at 1/2d per pound, liver 1/- and shoulder of mutton 1/3d and she will be glad to know why your prices are higher.
Yours faithfully.'

The private secretary received the following reply from Mrs Judd:

'Dear Sir
In reply to your enquiry with regard to prices. I beg your consideration of the enclosed market reports from which you will see that my charge is hardly even a reasonable profit on prime joints, considering the quantity of coarse meat which has to be sold below cost. Though the markets are very slightly easier than they have been it is not likely to be lasting. I do not think that Mr Snook's prices are less than mine to customers who deal solely with him. I am extremely sorry that Lady Radnor is dissatisfied and think if her Ladyship were to enquire of other ladies, it would be found that I charge no more than is paid in other towns in the south. Should the market prices during this

month allow I shall be glad to quote a reduction before my next
turn to supply the castle.
I am dear Sir, Yours faithfully.'

This correspondence batted back and forth for a while and the last letter
in the file is crossed through with what appears to be an angry swipe
of a red crayon. I do not know how the matter ended but have a feeling
that Mr Snook's accounts would have shown a comfortable increase
in turnover. In the meantime the officers and staff at Longford Castle
continued to be well fed and her ladyship extended hospitality to many
important and influential visitors!

I find no record of George V having ever been entertained by the
Earl and Countess despite a visit by the Prince of Wales earlier in the
war. He did, however, make frequent visits to the Plain to review his
armies, including those from Canada, Australia and New Zealand, as
reported by the *Journal* on a memorable occasion in early 1917:

'The presentation to the King of the Mayor of Salisbury at
Tuesday's review of the troops was not only a deserved
compliment to Mr Macklin for his public services during four
successive years in office, but a recognition of the City as a
military centre. His Majesty, in tones audible to the spectators
around the saluting base, thanked the Mayor for his personal
service, and through him the citizens for all they had done for
the soldiers. No one could possibly foresee the extent of the
organisations that now exist in Salisbury for the benefit of
soldiers – and their dependants also – and it is just as well that
fore knowledge was impossible, or it may be that the courage
that sustained the efforts, year after year, would have been
lacking. Perseverance in well-doing has been marked, and Royal
recognition cannot be other than gratifying to the Mayor and
others engaged in such work.'

Later in the year the king decided to change the name of the Royal
Family to Windsor and the *Journal* certainly approved by stating that,
'the decision of the King to change the name of his House and family
to Windsor and to relinquish all German titles has given unqualified
satisfaction throughout the British Empire.'

Her Majesty Queen Mary. (Taylor Library)

*His Majesty King George V. This portrait
hangs in the Guildhall, Salisbury. It was
painted by Frank Brooks and 'presented
to his native city' in 1918. (Salisbury City
Council)*

The *Journal's* leader of 21 July 1917 continued with what I regard
as a strange remark considering King George's own parents and
ancestry. It said: *'We hope that there will also be a return to the good
old British practice of the members of the Royal Family marrying
British women or British men.'* Perhaps the writer can be forgiven
considering the extreme hatred of anything German that was prevalent

by this stage of the war. A further report linking the Kaiser, King George's cousin, to Salisbury makes interesting reading:

> *'Many quaint stories of the amazing egotism of the Kaiser have been published since the WAR LORD ceased to have any claim upon the international courtesy that mercifully shielded his weaknesses. The latest emanating from Salisbury, is published in Major-General Sir George Younghusband's book:* A Soldier's Memories. *The story has its ridiculous side but a touch of the ridiculous is characteristic. During a visit to the City, Younghusband records that his Majesty rose in his motor car and addressed a crowd of boys in these stirring words: "Citizens of the town of Salisbury. I have just visited your beautiful and ancient Cathedral and my only sorrow is that I am not an Englishman that I may be a part owner of it", dropping tears the while at his own eloquence. It is certainly not the fault of the Kaiser that he has not become a part owner. Remembering the destruction of Rheims the circumstance becomes an added cause of thankfulness.'*

Kaiser Wilhelm II. (Taylor Library)

Or, at a colloquial level:

'When the war is over and we've captured Kaiser Billy,
To shoot him would be merciful and absolutely silly.
Just send him down to Larkhill amongst the mud and clay,
I bet it won't be long before he droops and fades away.'

Fading away – well not quite! By early 1917 the whole issue of feeding the nation had become of paramount importance. Lloyd George, himself, had said: 'The nation may have to choose between diminishing its military effort and underfeeding the population. There are only a few weeks in which to sow the spring wheat, the oats, the barley and the potatoes.'

Salisbury was fortunate, in that Captain Charles Bathurst, a frequent visitor to Longford and the Member of Parliament for South Wilts, had risen to the position of Parliamentary Secretary to the Ministry of Food and was in a position to pontificate on the subject, in no uncertain terms as reported by the *Journal* in the spring of 1917. Bathurst had attended the Royal Agricultural College at Cirencester (1895) where he won a scholarship with 98.5% of the possible marks.

'Captain Bathurst said that a great self-denying effort had now to be made by the whole civilian population of this country – a greater effort than it had ever made before or was ever likely to be called upon to make again. The great effort that had to be made by every section of the whole civilian population was an effort of self-denial in the matter of food. The most serious reason for the present shortage in breadstuffs was the increased scarcity of shipping. It was often erroneously stated that this was mainly due to enemy submarines. That was not the fact: it was mainly due to the fact that the larger proportion of British shipping was, today, occupied in carrying troops, weapons of war and foodstuffs, not only to our own armies abroad but to the armies of our allies (France and Italy) as well; but it was also due to an increased extent to that particular form of German savagery which was displayed by the activities of their submarines. The loss of shipping tonnage during the last three months had been very heavy as the result of enemy mines or

torpedoes, but particularly heavy during the last fortnight or three weeks, and one had, with some reluctance to confess that the skill of the enemy in this form of warfare was increasing, and we had so far been unable to devise any effect method of largely reducing the number of submarines.

Although there had been, speaking roughly, an average loss of about half a million tons of shipping each month, during the last three months, fortunately – and this was not generally known – the percentage of food cargoes that had been destroyed in this way was very small; but unfortunately it was increasing, and it was for that reason, as well as because the aggregate amount of shipping which was capable of carrying food in the future was becoming less, that the nation was being urged to use every possible economy in the matter of breadstuffs and particularly the avoiding of waste.'

Curiously, despite cessation of regular reports of casualties relating to the various theatres of war, the *Journal* started a weekly analysis of shipping losses broken down into statistics for ships over 1,600 tons, less than 1,600 tons and fishing boats. They also reported attacks that had failed to sink their target.

The report of Captain Bathurst's speech continued:

'He had no hesitation in saying that he was confident that the civilian population would, by their self-denial, ensure that neither the blood nor treasure of England had been poured out in vain, but would secure such a victory as would maintain the prestige of the British Empire, and would prevent anything like the horrors of this present war occurring again for at least a century.'

Echoing these sentiments, King George issued a proclamation, in May. He urged his subjects to exercise frugality as the surest means of defeating the enemy. Sir Derek Keppel, Master of the Household, added that His Majesty would never expect his people to sacrifice in a way that would not endure himself. *'We are all on strict rations here, and have been since the beginning of February'*, he said.

Perhaps a more earthy contribution was supplied by the Dean of

Salisbury when he said, 'wastefulness is a sin against humanity', or as someone else put it, 'every time we take a bigger helping, we are firing a shot for the Hun!'

However, the Lord Lieutenant of Wiltshire, Lord Lansdowne, decided to make an appeal for economy in a long letter to his people, published in the *Journal*, which I believe contains many of the elements that pre-occupied the populace at the time which is why it is reproduced here, in full. To my mind it also exemplifies a very English approach.

'I am invited to call the attention of my Wiltshire neighbours to the appeal which has been made to us all for economy in the consumption of food, and particularly of bread and breadstuffs.

Up to the present time the greater part of the community has not felt the real stress of war. Few families have indeed escaped from suffering of other kinds, and in this respect our own county has had its full share of sorrow. But it would probably be true to say that until now, although most of us have had to submit to a certain amount of discomfort and inconvenience owing to the war, nothing approaching privation has been experienced in any household.

Today the situation is rapidly changing. The failure of the staple crops at home and abroad, the appropriation of tonnage for purposes connected with the war, and, most serious of all, the heavy and increasing toll levied upon our shipping by the German submarines have brought us to a point at which a catastrophe might easily occur, and can only be avoided by an effort far more general, and far more determined, than any which we have yet been called upon to make.

How that effort can best be made we have been told in the speeches which have been recently delivered by responsible ministers and in the instructions that have been issued by the Food Controller's Department.

'It has been made clear to us that:

1. We should avoid waste, both in cooking and eating.

2. That we must restrict consumption.

3. That we must resort, whenever the circumstances permit, to the substitution of new articles of food to many of those to which we have been accustomed.

It has also been shown how necessary it is that the women of this country, who have a part to play not less important and not less honourable than that of the men who are fighting or working with us, should throw themselves into the enterprise, the success of which must depend mainly upon their whole-hearted co-operation. We are assured that, administered upon these lines, our visible resources will last until the new harvest comes in, bringing with it a temporary relief from the emergency.

But we cannot wait until the new harvest comes in to decide whether still more stringent measures are indispensable. It has been announced, wisely I think, that if our people will not ration themselves the Government will ration them. The machinery of compulsion is already being set up, and will be put in motion the moment it becomes clear that the voluntary system is going to fail.

"May not this", someone will say, "be, after all the fairest, and the most effective mode of arriving at the desired result?" The answer should, I am convinced, be in the negative – compulsion will certainly not be a simple remedy. The difficulty of imposing dietary restrictions on a free people by arbitrary methods would, in a community like ours, be immense. Such compulsion, implying as it would, bread tickets, domiciliary visits, and the creation of a new army of paid officials, whose visits must, of necessity, be inquisitorial and exasperating, would be detestable.

Compulsion would not work fairly, as between rich and poor, town and country. It has not worked smoothly in Germany, where it is notorious that it has exhausted the patience of a usually long-suffering population, and provoked bread riots and disturbances.

If, for no other reasons than these, I believe the bulk of our people will prefer to conform loyally, and of their own accord, to a scale laid down for their guidance by experts, and will feel, as Lord Devonport (Food Controller) has recently said, that "to win through on a voluntary system will be a national victory of we should all be proud".

The voluntary plan has this further advantage – it leaves room for the adjustments, the elasticity, the "give and take" which are essential to a reasonable arrangement, and for which there would be no room in a hard and fast code of Government regulations. It would, for example, be unfair from those who depend mainly on bread a sacrifice mathematically equal to that imposed upon those whose opportunities enable them to supplement their diet with other articles of food.

These questions of detail cannot be treated in such a letter as I am attempting to write, but committees have been set up in order to supply the necessary information, and the local councils will be asked to co-operate so that it should be possible for everyone in this county to obtain the necessary advice.

Numerous leaflets, full of sound and practical suggestions, have already been issued by the Food Controllers Department, and can easily be obtained from the local food committees which have been established in all districts by the War Savings Committee.

Only one word more – If anyone hesitates to make the sacrifice demanded of him, let him, if he has any sense of proportion, consider how it compares, which the sacrifice our own men have been called upon to make in the battlefields of France and Flanders, Gallipoli and Mesopotamia or, again with those to which the civil population of France and Belgium are submitting at the present moment. Our sacred edifices are intact, our great houses have stood as they have stood for centuries, our farmsteads and cottages are secure and peaceful, our soil is cultivated and we are all striving to obtain an increased return from it.

In order that these things may so remain, we are asked to reduce our weekly consumption of bread by at least 1lb per head. This, while we are only a few miles from a country whose churches and cathedrals are in ruins, whose historic houses are in the dust, of whose farms and cottages nothing remains but blackened rafters and crumbling walls, whose soil, enriched by generations of thrifty cultivation has been so scarred and wrecked that the features are no longer recognisable and its fertility is permanently destroyed.

With these considerations before us, surely there can be no room for hesitation.

I am, your obedient servant. LANSDOWNE. '

Other members of the Wiltshire community soon punched their weight in the pursuit of economy. In a letter from Breamore, Lady Edith Hulse, wrote as follows to the *Journal*:

> *'Sir, I venture to appeal to the citizens of Salisbury to strain every nerve…and to place themselves outside the prospective scheme of compulsory rationing. The Mayor's appeal at the recent meeting of the Town Council is indeed deserving of our warmest and most patriotic support. The honour of Salisbury is very dear to all of us. As the war record of Salisbury is a fine one, let us see to it that we do not fail in our bounden duty of helping to defeat the submarine strategy of our enemies by making our food*

Lady Edith Hulse: The first lady Mayor of Salisbury. This portrait, painted by Florence K Upton hangs in the Guildhall. It was presented by her brother Viscount Burnham CH. (Salisbury City Council)

supply outlast their activity. I appeal as one who is devoted to the interests of Salisbury and of her citizens, and who will be proud and glad if the city can add to her war record the honour and glory of voluntary rationing.
Yours very sincerely.'

Lady Hulse, whose son 'Ted' had been killed two years previously would, doubtless, have still been grieving.

Meanwhile Lieutenant Osmund Wordsworth, the son of the sub-dean of Salisbury Cathedral, who, with his sister had survived the sinking of the RMS *Lusitania* in 1915 was killed in action in France serving with the Machine Gun Corps on 2 April 1917. He has no known grave and his memory is recorded in Salisbury and on the Arras Memorial. The Wiltshire press noted that his life had been previously saved that he might sacrifice it *'for his men and for his sense of duty'.*

On Rogation Sunday, the Bishop of Salisbury, preaching from the pulpit, turned his attention to the rules laid down by the food controlling authorities. He made it clear that those who could afford to buy meat and other food should abstain from purchasing bread for the sake of their poorer brethren. I hope his own health did not suffer from lack of nutrition as it was reported, later in the year, that he had left the diocese for health reasons and 'only letters of pressing importance and

F.J .White's Ford delivering bread and buns. This photograph was probably taken soon after the Great War. (Peter Daniels)

those referring to bereavements in the diocese should be addressed to him'. On the subject of dietary discipline, another report in the local press echoed identical sentiments:

> *'The mass of the population must have bread. To the poor it is the chief necessity of life, for it is cheap and needs no cooking. Not only people of means, but those who at present are earning high wages, can afford to buy and cook other food. Let the cheaper foods – cheese, rabbits, the cheaper cuts of meat, the more popular kinds of fish – be left for those who cannot afford anything else. The rich can endure breadless days, the poor cannot.'*

So what practical steps were taken to follow the suggestions made? On a national front, various measures were introduced which included the guarantee of prices to farmers for wheat and oats, the freezing of rents, and every labourer, on the land, was guaranteed a minimum weekly wage of 25s. In the spring of 1917, it was noted that the stock of potatoes was extremely low and likely to remain so for a number of months. So bad was this situation that a farmer, some miles from Salisbury, was attacked by a group of fierce women and forced to part with his stock that had been destined for a market in Bristol. Normal supply and demand would have meant soaring prices so they were fixed by the Food Controller 'so as to keep potatoes within the reach of the poorer classes, to whom they are a necessity of life'.

Locally, Salisbury Council implemented the maximising of allotment cultivation and agreed that all vacant land should be turned over to horticulture and the production of foodstuffs. The Salisbury and Wilts Co-Operative Gardening Association became the Salisbury Land Cultivation Society Ltd. They clearly took to heart a notice that appeared in the local press headed:

> *'Your Garden and the Empire.*
> *In these days production is clearly linked up with patriotism and gardeners are urged by government to meet their output of vegetable foods to meet the Empire's needs.'*

One Salisbury firm enticed their customers with the words: '*Double your garden crops without extra cost. Twice as many delicious and nourishing vegetables*', and Messrs Woodrow and Co the ironmongers of Castle Street who rejoiced in the telephone number Salisbury 1 and the telegram address, IRON SALISBURY, advertised with the words:

> *'I am more cheerful since I started cultivating a plot of land. The submarine menace doesn't worry me nearly so much now, and my work is reduced to the minimum with the aid of Woodrow's good tools.*

Pig farming and poultry rearing was encouraged as reflected in the introduction of a weekly column in the *Journal* entitled, *'Poultry Notes (by an expert)'* although it was suggested that people should designate 'meatless days'.

At one session of the tribunal, a member, referring to a plea for exemption by a conscientious objector, remarked, 'I don't see why he should not be given some service in connection with cultivation of land in Salisbury.'

Soldiers, a farmer and women working on the land at Downton, near Salisbury, during the Great War. (Wiltshire Museum, Devizes)

Soldiers marching on Salisbury Plain during the Great War. (T.S. Crawford)

One of the most significant steps was, of course, the Women's Land Army, of whom it was said. '*It is hard, back aching work; though varied it has long hours of monotony; it is dirty work, is poorly paid and the accommodation is rough. In all these respects it is comparable with the work that the men folk are doing in the trenches.*' Exaggerated perhaps, although with all the practice bombardment, rifle training and trench digging that took place on the Plain the writer of these few words was not that far off the mark.

A huge advertisement was placed in the national press calling for, '*10,000 Women at Once*'.

They were offered:

- *A free outfit, high boots, breeches, overall and hat*
- *Maintenance during training and during term of employment*
- *Travelling expenses*
- *Wages – 18s per week, or the district rate, whichever is the higher*
- *Housing personally inspected and approved by the Women's County Committee of the Board of Agriculture*

- *Work on carefully selected farms*
- *Promotion – good work rewarded by promotion and higher pay*
- *Special facilities for settlement at home or overseas after the war*

Allotments were handed over to the women of Salisbury where soldier or sailor husbands were absent, serving the Empire. Nevertheless, it was agreed that children under the age of twelve should not work in agriculture. Women over the age of thirty eventually received the Parliamentary Franchise under the Representation of the People Act: 1918.

Further encouragement in economy was supplied by The Goldfish, an established restaurant around the corner from Winchester Street. They reproduced comments that had appeared in the *Daily Telegraph* with regard to the Food Regulations: *'Frequenters of restaurants who have made a special study of war-time cookery can obtain many hints in food economy and how to prepare food to its best advantage.'*

The Goldfish also informed their customers that they would be very pleased to provide advice or help them in any way to introduce the new cooking in their home, despite regretting that they were unable to supply many of their retail customers with particular cakes they much desired. This was because the Food Controller had not 'granted us any sugar for cake making'.

Fred Sutton, the Salisbury bakers and pastry cooks asked their customers if they had tried Drueda – *'a bread made from the best flour and similar to the old fashioned home-made bread'*. They continued by quoting *The Lancet* which said, *'Drueda is of excellent texture and of good flavour. It shows a nourishing value decidedly in excess of that of ordinary white bread.'*

Heading in the same direction, despite being on an entirely different tack, a letter from Harnham, Salisbury is of interest:

'Sir, As an allotment holder I have read with interest your reports of the scheme to open up undeveloped land for allotments; also the scheme to supply seed potatoes to the holders.

While this scheme is being organised I would like to draw attention to the ever increasing difficulty of obtaining stable

Winchester Street in 1916. A McDonalds fast food outlet can be found on the left-hand side of the street today (2015). (Peter Daniels)

manure in quantities suitable for allotments. Can some enterprising person suggest a means whereby some of the large quantity available at the camps could be delivered to allotment holders at a reasonable charge and so encourage men to get all they possibly can out of their ground by good cultivation.
Yours truly, W. ADAMSON'

In horrific contrast, an account appeared in the Wiltshire press that the Germans were using the bodies of their men killed on the Western Front for the production of oil, pig's food and manure. The name of the chemical factory where this process was said to be enacted was, 'The Corpse Exploitation Establishment'. Hardly able to credit the truth of this report – and I fully understand that – the correspondent verified that it had appeared in the *Berliner Lokal-Anzeiger* and that those Germans who were aware of the process regarded it as 'a quite ordinary and commonplace matter'.

Easter came and went in that austere year of 1917 with little jollity. A symptom of malaise may have been that the men's outfitters, Charles H. Baker of Milford Street, Salisbury, abandoned their seasonal practice

Charles H. Baker on the corner of Milford Street and Brown Street as it is today (2015) with the Cathedral Hotel – where Lord Peter Wimsey lunched in Dorothy L. Sayers' novel 'Whose Body?' – rising above the shops. (NGMH)

Advertisement for Roper and Company, the military tailors and outfitters, that appeared regularly during the Great War in the Salisbury and Winchester Journal. *(Richard Broadhead)*

of supplying a glass of sherry together with simnel cake to their customers or to the carriers who brought in orders for dungarees, boiler suits and such like from the outlying farms. I am reliably informed on this matter by Robert Baker, whose grandfather started the business in 1902 and who is still involved in the running of the firm.

There was, however, some good news in the air!

After much deliberation – it is worth remembering that there was a huge German and German-speaking population in America – and mainly as a consequence of the unrestricted targeting of neutral shipping by German submarines, the United States declared war on Germany. In fact, before formal declaration, a state of war already existed following the sinking of three American ships.

David Lloyd George who became Prime Minister of Great Britain in 1916. (Taylor Library)

The Prime Minister Lloyd George declared: 'I can see peace coming now, not a peace which would be the beginning of war, not a peace which would be an endless preparation for strife and bloodshed, but a real peace.' Did Churchill have these words in mind with his famous speech some twenty-five years later, which strikes one as appropriate, even in 1917: 'This is not the end. It is not even the beginning of the end. But it is, perhaps, the end of the beginning.'

What the Kaiser expected to achieve by forcing this huge and powerful trans-Atlantic country into war is mystifying and as one of the New York newspapers commented at the time *'the recklessness of madmen, and the depravity of irreclaimable criminals'*.

Our own *Journal* looked to the future with optimism: *'The Allies will (also) receive great aid by the supply of ships, food, munitions and money. If there was ever a doubt as to the result of the war, it will disappear with the decision of the United States to take a share in avenging the awful crimes committed by Germany against humanity.'*

The first American troops arrived in France on 26 June 1917. Shortly after this the *Journal* commented that the Americans, now under the leadership of General Pershing, would give the Germans a rude shock and even surprise the British with their resources, energy and idealism. In fact, the *Journal* could be accused of waxing somewhat lyrical as this passage, describing the American people suggests:

'While they have obtained all the best characteristics of the Anglo-Saxon race, they have acquired new virtues which make them the most intelligent, inventive, industrious people of the earth. Is there any other nation where women hold the same honoured position as in the United States? As to their vast power and resources of every kind, have we not recently been given evidence of them in the subscriptions for the Liberty Loan and in the contributions for the Red Cross Fund? In three years, with gigantic efforts, the whole British Empire has raised rather more than seven million pounds sterling by voluntary contributions for the Red Cross. The people of the United States gave over twenty million pounds sterling for the same object in one week!'

Back in the spring, Captain Bathurst had referred to the 'treasure of England'. Besides allotments and agriculture, poultry rearing and pig farming there was the perennial question of money and sufficient money to maintain the war effort. Early in the year a meeting was held in the council chamber to which all businessmen and farmers were invited. They were addressed by Arthur Marshall MP on, 'The Urgent Need for Everyone Subscribing to the New War Loan'; with James Macklin, the mayor, in the chair. The leader in the *Journal* spelled out the details:

'The new War Loan is a magnificent investment. Its security is the British Empire – the best in the world. The rate of interest is five per cent, and the price of issue is £95 for every £100 of Loan so that the yield to the investor is almost five and one quarter per cent. The small investor will obtain all the benefits which can be obtained by the rich capitalist.'

Further details were supplied before the leader continued:

'The Loan will be for a period of thirty years, the State reserving the right to redeem it at par at the end of twelve years. Here is an opportunity for everyone to aid the Empire, to win the war and at the same time to make a profitable investment. We are confident the nation as a whole, will make a response which will

both hearten and cheer the men who are fighting for us, and show the enemy how united and determined we are to fight on until victory is won. Every subscription to the new Loan is a blow struck at Germany.'

Indeed, on the last day that subscription to the loan was possible (16 February 1917), huge advertisements appeared in the press screaming out:'HAVE YOU INVESTED IN THE WAR LOAN? – GERMANY IS WATCHING US.'

The drive for the War Loan proved a success. Half a million pounds sterling, was invested in Salisbury alone. With regard to further savings – the idea seemed to be catching on – one, H.N. Devenish, a businessman from Little Durnford, near Salisbury, wrote: '*At Little Durnford, I gave all my employees a 15/6d certificate and in order to encourage thrift, promised them 2/- on each further 15/6d they saved. I have started the War Savings Cards, taken up at Great Durnford with six pence each.*'

There was, of course, another side to the coin (no pun intended). As compared with prices recorded in August 1916 the increase in the price of principal articles of food was something in the region of twenty per cent, a year later. Different foodstuffs had attracted a huge range of increases – the average was about seventy-five per cent from the start of the war in 1914, after eliminating the rises brought on by increased taxation. In late October 1917 the Board of Trade increased the price of coal to half a crown (2s 6d) per ton and the Salisbury Gas Light and Coke Company increased the price of gas to 3s 5d per 1,000 cubic feet. In Salisbury, the *Journal* was once again forced to increase the price of its weekly edition because of the increased price of raw materials and a notice was posted prohibiting tradesmen from publishing catalogues for the same reason.

Meanwhile fundraising and the drive for economy continued. The Godolphin School raised £860 at a superb garden sale which was donated to Queen Mary's Needlework Guild (£500) and the Red Cross (£360) and regular lists of donors appeared in the local press. A typical example, in one edition, was a list of thirty generous citizens who had given flowers, eggs, vegetables, potatoes, magazines, books, jam, bandages, cakes and buns to the poor, hospitals and other needy recipients. In the autumn, it was suggested by the Salisbury Education

St Mark's school as it is today (2015) – converted to private flats. (NGMH)

Committee that boys should collect horse chestnuts (conkers) and that these should be sent to munitions factories as the chestnuts contained certain properties required in the manufacture of armaments that would otherwise need to be extracted from wheat. Close supervision was recommended as 'boys will be boys', in this, the ultimate economy and utilisation of free and natural resources.

War or no war the boys of Salisbury were, indeed, boys as the headmaster of St Mark's school logged on 26 October: *'The attendance has been broken and poor. Largely, no doubt, due to the fair on Monday, Tuesday and Wednesday.'*

At Enford, not far from Salisbury, E.B. Maton took to ploughing grassland on the Plain, much aided by the new tractors built by the Austin Motor Company of Birmingham and attracting an article by a special correspondent of the *Daily Mail*, entitled A SALISBURY

PRAIRIE. *'Every shipload of oats I can produce will release a ship to bring human food or munitions to our country,'* Maton had said, despite finding himself at the heart of controversy relating to Sunday working, upon which topic both the Archbishop and the Bishop of Salisbury were required to pronounce. Although not working on a Sunday was deeply ingrained in the culture at the time, many were prepared to shake off this restriction in view of the national emergency. The primates had sanctioned working on the Sabbath providing that it was really necessary and at Enford – a case of 'if Mohammed won't come to the mountain', perhaps – two local clergymen conducted a remarkable service among the men employed in the fields – 'fighting in the furrows'.

One requirement for oats was to feed the horses and in a detailed letter to the *Journal* from the secretary of the Salisbury branch of the RSPCA, precise rationing (The Horses Rationing Order), as stipulated by the Food Controller was outlined: *'For instance, horses used for trade or business purposes may receive a daily oat ration, varying from sixteen pounds for heavy horses to seven pounds for ponies ... .'*

Meanwhile, advertisements, placed by the local recruiting office, appeared in Salisbury seeking men between the ages of forty-one and sixty, who had experience with horses. They might be jockeys, hunt servants, coachmen, grooms, strappers or carriers and they were required for the Army Service Corps, Remount Depot.

'Men may be enlisted under the following conditions' – the notices continued: *'For the duration of the war – Weight not to exceed 14 stone – Not to be ruptured or suffering from anything which would prevent equitation – Height and eyesight immaterial.'*

Horses and the care of horses permeated the way of life in Wiltshire one hundred years ago which is why these few lines, penned by one, Louisa Willcox must have struck a chord in 1917.

She said: *'Today, for you and my father who love horses so much, I have visited a big hospital for horses and I am glad to have done so, for I never expected to find anything so wonderful. It is a Receiving Hospital straight from the Front, the wounded and the sick had just arrived; they were being fed and watered and their wounds most beautifully dressed, the men are so gentle with them.'*

Louisa continued with further detail and concluded: *'All the men I spoke to were horse lovers and just love looking after them. It is so sad these dear animals have to suffer so. I did so want to tell them how sad I felt for them.'*

Saddlery businesses would have flourished in Wiltshire during the Great War but having contacted Marlborough based, David Chandler, a past Master of The Worshipful Company of Saddlers, and having relayed my enquiry to the archivist of that organisation, no records have been forthcoming.

The nearest that I have come in my quest is to talk to the current and very helpful proprietor of Ingrams in Catherine Street, who were originally saddlers in nearby Codford, although they moved to the city in 1923 and now trade in luggage and leather goods, and also to Mark Romain who, together with his wife, runs a remarkably well attended international saddlery school near the railway station. However, with no trading or personnel details available I am forced to conclude that people at the time just did not think it important to retain the minutiae of their trade. What a shame!

Saddlery aside, the Romsey Remount Depot, situated twenty miles to the south-east of Salisbury, whose prime function was to train horses and mules for war service, dealt with more than a million animals during the course of the war. These wretched creatures, of which half were imported from North America, were processed at Romsey and various camps including one at Swaythling which is between Salisbury and Southampton.

There was, of course, little let up in the number of casualties in all theatres of war. Every time news of a casualty reached Salisbury, be it a death, a wounded man or a prisoner, a wide circle of family, friends, businesses and other communities would be affected. Private Wilfred Anson, who was killed at Passchendaele and whose parents lived in the Close and were connected to the Cathedral, is an example, as was Private B. Lever who had worked for Style and Gerrish and whose brother had previously died in Mesopotamia.

Private William A. Grace, a former employee of Messrs Brown, the booksellers of The Canal, Salisbury also represents those formerly involved with trade in the city. Mrs Ada Grace received the following from her husband's commanding officer – perhaps a typical communication that landed on the doormat of many properties during those grim days:

Passchendaele: wounded lie around a block house near the site of Zonnebeke railway station in October 1917. (Taylor Library)

'I fear my news can be only of a negative character. Your husband went over the top with the company on the night of April 24th and 25th, but did not return after the assault, nor was he found by our subsequent search parties. I am afraid, therefore, that he must have been killed when we were held up in the Bulgar wire, or got through and was killed in the enemy *trenches. We have received names of very few who were taken prisoner by the enemy on this occasion, but unfortunately your husband's name does not occur. Your husband, "Gracie", as he was known to all of us, was in my platoon before I took over the Company, and was most popular with us all, being always eager and willing to do his job and give anybody all the assistance that in his power lay. His comrades will mourn a good soldier gone to rest. Permit me, madam, to offer you, on behalf of his comrades and myself, our profound condolence and sympathy in your bereavement.'*

When 19-year-old Guardsman, Thomas Witt died, probably of wounds sustained at the Battle of Cambrai, his parents of Park Street, Salisbury added these words to the announcement:

'We do not know what pain he bore,
We never saw him die,
We only know he passed away
And never said goodbye.'

Not all news was sombre. Regular items reporting military decorations featured in the Salisbury press including Captain G.A. Parker, the son of J. L. Parker of Castle Street whose awards of the DSO and MC were announced on the same day. In August 1917 Captain Charles Bathurst MP was appointed Chairman of the Royal Commission on Sugar Supply and was honoured as Knight Commander of the Order of the British Empire. This was regarded as significant as this new order was the first of its kind to be available to both men and women.

Wiltshire folk were in the lucky position of being able to drink their Member's success with the newly licensed 'Light Harvest Ale', supplied by John Lovibond and Sons of the city. I hope they drank well and were merry as the harvest that year, the third anniversary of the start of the war, was later than usual. After a severe winter and cold spring, the sowing of spring corn had been delayed and coupled with the scarcity of skilled labour there was much anxiety in the farming community. However, all was eventually gathered in, precipitating a delayed harvest festival. The brew was especially sanctioned by the Food Controller so they must have had enough sugar.

Whether in their cups or not, the Salisbury press was never short of news of a more international nature. Early in 1917 came a report from Salisbury, Rhodesia of the compulsory registration of all males so that a ledger could be compiled of those suitable for military service in support of the Motherland and Empire.

In August, news of the Imperial Russian family's departure from Tsarskoe Selo to a remote region of Russia, accompanied by members of the Bolshevik government and a military guard, made ominous reading. Four months later, a further report related that the Russian Fifth Army had sworn allegiance to Lenin – probably in the pay of the Germans – it was suggested. An armistice was signed on 2 December at 10pm.

As the year began to draw to a close news of a mutiny of the German navy at Kiel and the entry of Jerusalem by Allenby must surely have raised morale. Perhaps the end of the conflict really was in sight but Christmas in Salisbury, that year was not a jolly occasion. Few Christmas cards were sent and the prospect of compulsory rationing cast a dark shadow over the populace.

A letter appeared in the *Journal* requesting toys to be collected for the benefit of poor children. It was placed by Percy James Southon,

The 1ˢᵗ Salisbury (YMCA) Scout Troop at Harnham in 1910. Percy James Southon, sits on the right with arms folded. He survived military service in the Great War and some years later was awarded the MBE for services to Salisbury youth. (Peter Daniels)

who, in 1907 founded Southons, the furniture store that still trades in Catherine Street, ably managed by his grandson, Chris. Percy, who inaugurated the Salisbury Scouts, went to the war and returned safely. Some years later he was awarded the MBE for services to Salisbury youth. His photograph is displayed in the furniture showroom.

The letter concluded with the rider that broken toys should also be given, as they could probably be fixed.

It was good to read that those old playthings might be mended. But what about the broken hearts and lives, the shattered minds and the splintered bones that were evident in Salisbury during that December of 1917? Could they ever be repaired?

CHAPTER 5

1918
Pigs, Potatoes and Brighter Prospects

I was fortunate to be invited to meet Ethel Towl (née Chant) in the autumn of 2014. Armed with a large bunch of chrysanthemums, I drove to Shrewton, on the Plain, where she was still living in the pretty Edwardian house where she had been born in 1912. Her hearing was not good although her mind was incisive. Following an introduction by her niece and once pleasantries had been exchanged, I asked her what she recalled of the Great War. 'I remember Uncle Albert,' she replied. 'He worked in the family bakery business, here in Shrewton, and went to France but never came back, along with eleven other men from our village. It was only after the Armistice that we heard what had happened to him. Usually we got news of the war from the carriers who plied their trade with Salisbury and the surrounding villages. We had three Australian officers billeted in one of the rooms upstairs. They wore funny wide-brimmed hats and mother had to cook a meal for them every night – they were very polite and kind.'

Australians had not always lived up to the glowing praise that came from Ethel's lips and as I drove away, after tea, I recalled reports of disturbances on the streets of Salisbury and elsewhere. However, a letter which appeared in the *Journal* in 1918 throws further interesting light on the Australian invasion.

Ethel Towl in her home at Shrewton (2015), which was where she was born in 1912. (Ken Jones)

H.L. Chant's Supply Stores in Shrewton at the beginning of the Great War. (Ken Jones)

'Dear Sir, We write to thank you and the hospitable people of Salisbury for your kindness to our Australian boys. At the call of duty our best and bravest from university, from warehouse and from the bush, cheerfully stepped forward and offered themselves.

Our adopted boy, C. Hedberg, wrote in glowing terms of his gratitude to the people of your city… .

My two sisters in Manchester wrote him, and he promised, before going to France, to spend his leave with them, but a sudden call came, and he was hurried to France and never saw them. After three big fights, he entered his fourth on March 13th, was struck by a shell, and passed away in a moment.

He now quietly rests on Messines Ridge, but please God, we shall meet him again some day and, we trust too, all the Salisbury friends who in such a kindly, thoughtful way, did their best to help our boys from many a good home in Australia… .
Yours gratefully
Joseph and Isabella Whalley
Canterbury, Australia.'

'Australia' etched on the chalk down land at Hurdcott Park. (T.S. Crawford)

There would be other invasions. In June 1918, Bonar Law announced in the Commons: 'The Americans are not coming; they have come!'

Lord Lansdowne appealed for Wiltshire folk to get together, to provide hospitality and entertainment for our American friends. The

Journal reported that *'he hoped that the question would be taken up enthusiastically by the public because they must recognise that they owed a deep debt of gratitude to the Americans for stepping into the breach in the way they had.'*

In June 1918 the *Journal* further reported a meeting in the council chamber, *'with a view to enlisting sympathy in a movement for the extension of hospitality to American soldiers stationed in the neighbourhood of Salisbury.'* The Mayor, James Macklin remarked that *'the citizens of Salisbury had already shown their deep sense of gratitude to their other friends – the Canadians, Australians and New Zealanders – and given proof that they are a hospitable city, and he was sure their attitude towards the Americans would be quite as cordial.'*

He was right, and it would not be long before baseball charity matches would be played between rival US Aero Squadrons in Victoria Park, in the heart of the city!

I am sure that all this must have cheered everyone up because my abiding impression, while undertaking research, is that by 1918 the population of Salisbury and probably the whole country was suffering from extreme exhaustion and traumatic stress. Perhaps, nowhere more than at the Archdeacon's home in the Close, where news of the death of Captain Charles Hodgson, his son-in-law, would soon be received. As I have already recorded, Archdeacon Carpenter had lost his son on the Somme in 1916. Hodgson died of wounds and is buried in the Cairo War Memorial Cemetery, Egypt, as is my great-uncle Lieutenant G.V. Oldrey.

Salisbury Cathedral cloisters: a temporary cross marking the death of Captain C.B.M Hodgson in Cairo on 1 April 1918. (NGMH)

Today, some items of news might appear amusing although at the time they probably reflected a life pitted with mild irritations. Under the Defence of the Realm Act it became illegal to manufacture ladies' high leg boots. Why should this be? Probably because the army needed all available leather. Messrs Moore Brothers, the Salisbury Military and Family Bootmakers, were happy to oblige with a small stock of their own manufacture.

Contravening the Public Meats Order – restrictions designating 'meatless' days – a man was prosecuted for taking a cold partridge into a restaurant and attempting to consume it. Another man was also summoned before the beak, and fined £1 for stealing six chickens, although policemen more often than not, turned a blind eye when spotting, possibly hungry, children scrumping apples. Following the rationing of coal and the appointment of Fuel Overseers this note appeared in the *Journal* – amusing or maddening?

'With the appointment of Fuel Overseers, householders are beginning to look for some definition as to what constitutes a "room". It is well known that the coal will be rationed according to the number of rooms occupied – ranging in Wiltshire from three tons for two rooms to eleven tons for twelve rooms; and for every additional room one ton is allowed to a maximum of twenty tons.'

The article continues to try and throw light on the situation and define a '*room*' with reference to attics, pantries, sculleries, bathrooms, halls, box-rooms, cellars and so on. It certainly gave the Bishop of Salisbury a monumental headache so he vacated his palace.

Eventually compulsory rationing was introduced. Sugar was rationed in January 1918 and by April, meat, butter, margarine and cheese had also been restricted. The king and queen were not exempt from receiving ration cards which were issued to everyone.

Allowances per week were as follows:

15oz of meat
5oz of bacon
4oz of butter or margarine
1½oz of tea
8oz of sugar

Everyone had to register with a butcher for meat, a different retailer for bacon, a dairy for butter and margarine, a sugar retailer and a general store.

The Maypole Dairy of Silver Street, Salisbury, reminded their customers that they were free to register with which ever firm they preferred. They announced in a full page advertisement in the local press that the Food Controller urged them to register with the shopkeeper who gave them the *MOST* and *BEST* for their housekeeping money. *'Remember too, that NO Retailer may offer you any inducement, direct or indirect, to register with them.'* They implored.

With the shortages of food and what the *Journal* now referred to as The Hun Piracy, when reporting shipping losses in its weekly column, there was no let up in efforts to control the food supply. The *Journal* even ran a weekly column entitled *'Our Food Supply'* and the Haunch of Venison, one of the better known hostelries in Salisbury, and indeed Wessex, was compelled to close their grill room. It was even suggested that a communal kitchen be instigated in Salisbury although this does not appear to have occurred. The feeding of animals was also to be supervised. Late in 1918 the Live Stock Commissioner for the Ministry of Food now required Forms of Application for a licence to purchase feeding stuff for cattle, horses and pigs.

Potatoes and pigs remained a major topical issue. In March the local press featured huge notices exclaiming that in 1917, only 19,200 tons of potatoes had been produced in Wiltshire, while 26,900 tons had been consumed. Against this deficit (7,700 tons) an appeal was launched for *'every man who has a farm, a garden or an allotment to PLANT MORE POTATOES.'* As always, coming to the rescue in a crisis Charles Bathurst launched a scheme to raise money for assistance in this cause and Salisbury Council, also keen to assist in this 'work of national importance' devised plans for a municipal piggery in Salisbury. Again, I'm not sure if this actually worked but Bathurst had a reputation for putting his money where his mouth was and continued to make generous contributions for various causes! Sadly, over enthusiasm for moving pigs around on Salisbury Plain, resulted in a tragic accident when sixty-two pigs died while being transported in a rail truck. The railway company and consignor were heavily fined for causing death by overcrowding.

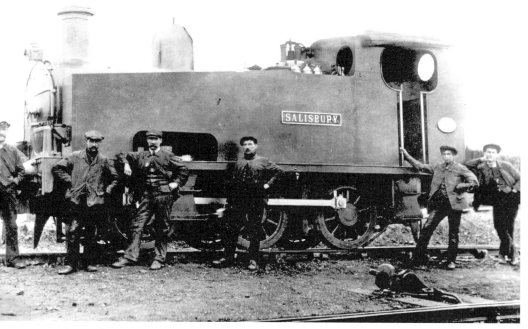

Steam locomotive 'Salisbury' at Larkhill during the Great War. (Wiltshire and Swindon History Centre)

In the pursuit of the production of further food some confusion – clearly unforeseen – arose with regard to local, Wiltshire 'shoots' and the disposal of game. The following piece from the *Journal* sheds some light on the issue:

> *'Briefly stated, the conditions laid down by the Food Controller are that owners and occupiers of "shoots" may make unfettered gifts of game to Red Cross and other hospitals, but other game – leaving out of account rabbits and hares to the "self-supplier", i.e. the owner or occupier – have to be accounted for by coupons cancelled from the meat cards of the self-supplier and of friends to whom gifts are made. The exact coupon rate is given in another column. A considerable onus is thrown upon the owner or occupier of keeping records for four-weekly periods showing the number of birds of each kind consumed in own household and supplied to hospitals and persons outside the household.*

Not all the questions of the Food Controller are answered. For instance there is no direction as to how a shooting party may journey to the "shoot" by car or otherwise. It is to be presumed, in the absence of directions, that guests at shooting parties must take their own rations, while there is no direction upon the custom of providing food for beaters, who presumably must also provide for themselves. But though every question is not definitely answered, the directions will be of value to many in district where shooting occurs.'

Clear as mud?

Despite all this, a short note in the *Journal* reported early success in the ration process and concluded that *'the prevailing impression is that while food shortages last rationing is infinitely preferable to the queue habit –* [apparently spawned during the Great War] *– and to the occasional unseemly scramble that took place.'*

Did the good people of Salisbury have any fun to counter these pressing considerations? I think they did, although a series of Lenten addresses in the Cathedral under the heading 'The Church and National Life' and given by the headmasters of three famous public schools (Marlborough, Wellington and Charterhouse) did not quite fit that bill. Certainly reports indicated that attendance was not what had been expected or hoped for. Perhaps the audience at the Picture House preferred to see Montagu Love in 'Rasputin or the Power behind the Throne', attracted by the programme that described the Russian as one well versed in the lore of mysticism who used his influence to diabolical purpose. The film, it was stated, gave demonstrations of his extraordinary power and its evil results.

In 1918 there was certainly always plenty to see at the theatres and cinemas in Salisbury and, of course, there were numerous concerts in aid of the wounded or bereaved as well. The efforts of Charlie Chaplin were commonplace but many of the titles would be unfamiliar to today's audience. However, the 1909 rendition of 'Napoleon – Man of Destiny', 'Lady Windermere's Fan' and 'Home Sweet Home' may well strike bells. And who could resist 'The Birth of a Nation' (1915) with 5,000 distinct scenes, 12,000 people and 3,000 horses?

While occupied in research I was surprised to find that in June,

Albany Ward – at the Picture House – was showing 'The Crisis – A magnificent drama founded on Winston Churchill's well known book'. Once again the audience was enticed by an explanation which stated that the film lasted for two and a half hours and was 'one of the finest productions of modern times'.

Other productions followed throughout the year including 'The Life of Lord Kitchener', 'The War at First Hand' (under the auspices of the Ministry of Information) which claimed to be 'the finest war film ever produced' and 'My Four Years in Germany', a series of films produced by a former US ambassador in Berlin.

Something of a novelty was a fascinating series of war pictures exhibited before open-air audiences in Salisbury and the surrounding area. The tour was arranged by the Ministry of Information and consisted of fully equipped apparatus, mounted on an ordinary army truck and accompanied by a speaker, an operator and a driver. As reported in the *Journal*: '*The pictures filmed show what our men are doing in the Army, the Navy and the Air Service, what munition workers have done, and how women are helping to win the war.*' The Market Square in Salisbury was, of course, an excellent venue for such an event.

Seeking frivolity, Salisbury folk attended Albany Ward's Palace Theatre to witness the first visit of the 'Bam Bams – America's Real Cowboys', and 'Marcelle de Vere – the Cycling Violinist'. More seriously, at the Salisbury City Petty Assizes, the RSPCA prosecuted a member of the circus for cruelty to a performing chimpanzee. Replying to the accusation that he thrashed the animal he said: 'It is impossible to train an animal by thrashing him because you would break his heart... .' Case dismissed.

On 4 August 1918 the fourth anniversary of the declaration of war fell on a Sunday. An appeal for more parcels for prisoners was launched and the Bishop called for all to attend services of Remembrance. At

36   HURDCOTT HERALD.

ALBANY WARD'S

PALACE

HURDCOTT CAMP

5-50   TWICE NIGHTLY   7-30

STAR TURNS

BEST PICTURES

SPECIAL ATTRACTIONS as Periodically Announced

Cosy Building, Amply Ventilated and Heated.

POPULAR PRICES.

BEST & QUICKEST

PRINTING

THE

SALISBURY PRESS

5 WILTON ROAD, SALISBURY

Advertising Albany Ward's 'Star Turns' at the Palace: Hurdcott Camp.

this stage, the Dean's words, in the Cathedral, make interesting reading:

'I pray your earnest attention. What right have we to expect that God will help us? Our German enemies pray for success and sing their hymns. Why should God hear us and not hear them? Because God is the supreme righteousness and because the cause for which we are fighting is a righteous one, and therefore in this respect we are one with God.'

Doing God's work, eh? Be that as it may, the report of a wedding at nearby Nunton records Wagner and Mendelsohn's music at the ceremony. The bridegroom, best man and another supporter were all hobbling around on crutches. All victims of the war – the latter had lost a leg on the Western Front. Being English, I am sure they viewed the situation with lashings of humour and self-deprecation.

One might think that the population of Salisbury were preoccupied with feeding themselves, being entertained and following the progress of the war but they also continued to be generous with their time and money. In the summer of 1918 a list of twenty-eight ladies, *'mentioned*

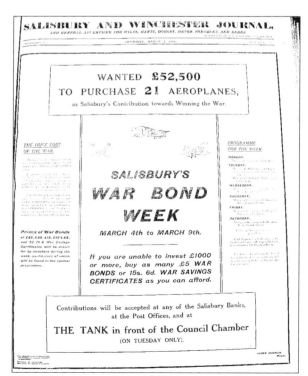

March 1918: advertisement placed in the Salisbury and Winchester Journal, *encouraging investment during 'War Bond Week'. (Richard Broadhead)*

Army tank brought into the Market Place for War Bond Week in March 1918. (Wiltshire and Swindon History Centre)

in despatches, for valuable nursing services in connection with the war', was published in the *Journal*. Subsequently a list of sixteen officers, stationed in Wiltshire Hampshire and Dorset, whose names had been brought to the attention of the Secretary of State for War *'for valuable service in connection with the war'* was published. A selection of Hospital Workers' names was also forwarded to the War Office with the same commendation.

In 1918 the war was costing the nation five million pounds per day and in the spring a huge drive to raise cash was launched. Many towns and cities across the country were provided with targets and in Salisbury War Bond Week the target set was £52,000 to purchase twenty-one aeroplanes. Magnificently, Salisbury raised £102,500 which was sufficient to add twenty-one planes and ten tanks to the nation's arsenal. Apparently, Salisbury's investment had exceeded all other towns in the West Country 'similarly circumstanced', with one significant (Winchester) and one minor (Weymouth) exception. It would not surprise me to know that the king's visit to Salisbury, later in the year, was partly arranged – he also inspected the Artillery and Royal

Engineer Schools in Southern Command – as a token of thanks for the city's financial contribution. It was also to express gratitude to the mayor and citizens 'for their sustained efforts in the public service and particularly for the welfare of the numerous troops visiting the city'. James Macklin, the mayor, was presented to King George who was greeted by wildly cheering children and the local populous as he drove through the city. According to the local press the guard was furnished by the Military Police, representatives of Southern Command and members of the United States Corps. Macklin was soon to be elected as mayor once more, the first citizen to be elected mayor for six consecutive years since 1300.

Down the road from the London and South Western Railway Station, where the presentation had taken place, life at the Infirmary continued very much as in previous years. An additional laundry allowance had been granted to the staff – a rise of 5s from 30s per week – salaries were increased, supplying sufficient food was a continuing headache and a chicken run was constructed on the property. I hope the management team were reading their '*Poultry Notes*': '*With so much frosty weather about it is necessary that the breeding stock be*

The clock tower and the Infirmary in Fisherton Street, Salisbury, during the time of the Great War. (Ken Jones)

well cared for and enough food supplied... . Fowls must not be allowed to get cold, for they soon mope around and look wretched.' Just like their hospital patients!

The copiously documented management meetings recorded shoals of wounded arriving from the front. As noted by Anthony Seldon and David Walsh in *Public Schools and the Great War*, it is often assumed that the fighting quietened down in 1918 although this is very far from the truth. The authors state that *'loss of life, including public school casualties, [it] was as devastating as the previous two [years].'* They continue: *'In only ten separate months throughout the war did the number of officer deaths exceed 1,100; five of those months fell in 1918, with August being the worst month of the whole war for officer deaths.'*

Fatal casualties throughout the war, as documented by Richard Broadhead in *Salisbury Soldiers*, were as follows:

1914: 26
1915: 67
1916: 112
1917: 127
1918: 158

At the Infirmary cases of typhoid, diphtheria, mumps, scarlet fever, German measles, whooping cough, appendicitis and – late in 1918 – the first mention of influenza which had confined twenty-five members of staff to their beds, were recorded. Then there was always the vexed subject of VD concerning which the authorities remained very coy. In my view this is understandable and reflects one of the undesirable impacts of the war upon a quiet market town. The entrance to the Skin Department was to be at a side entrance and a notice in the porter's office directed potential patients to Crane Bridge Road. Salisbury was not the only city affected, as is made clear by a directive from The National Council for Combating Venereal Disease which read: *'False shame is sheer folly. The doctor is not there to blame but to cure. Do not be frightened of going to the doctor – be frightened of the disease... .'*

Financial juggling was clearly a matter of vital importance. However, this was tempered by humanity and the call of duty. In October '18 the house surgeon reported *'that a convoy of ten soldiers had arrived, most of them being severely wounded. Three more were sent by mistake (they were intended for Cardiff) but on account of their serious injuries they were retained.'*

In contrast, I was amused to see an entry requesting the purchase of twelve fish knives and forks for the nurses' dining room. Granted.

The Infirmary was continually receiving gifts and bequests. In early 1918 a valuable consignment of medical supplies was received from the United States together with a gift of 200 'pyjama suits' for the soldiers. In contrast, because the army would not play ball, a grant of three pounds was made to one, Lance-Corporal Bradley for artificial dentures, on discharge from his regiment following an amputation. Bequests of investment stock more often than not remained invested to derive income as follows:

£600 India 3.5% stock
£2,000 India 3% stock
£2,000 New Zealand 4% stock (1943-1963)
£2,000 East Indian Railway 4.5% inscribed stock
£1,000 Madras Southern Mahratta 4% debenture stock

Various annuities:
Victoria 4% 1918 & 1922
Cape of Good Hope 4% 1923
Western Australia 4% 1942-1962

Despite fiscal prudence, the war and the effects of the war were never far away. Wounded soldiers, sailors and airmen arrived; some died, others were discharged and returned as out-patients. The question of re-imbursement of that particular expense to the Infirmary was a matter of debate with the authorities. A probationer nurse received news that her brother had been blown to bits in France and the introduction of ration cards added further administrative complications. All the sweeps had gone to the front so there was no-one to clean the chimneys and who was going to wind and service the seventeen clocks in the building? Only after extensive advertising in the *Guardian* and the raising of the age limit was a new (ineligible) chaplain appointed in 1918. To paraphrase the words of Edith Oliver – the war very visibly regulated the lives of the Infirmary and other hospitals in Wiltshire and elsewhere.

Meanwhile the work of the tribunals rumbled on.

Desmond Pye-Smith of the Close, Salisbury had volunteered for Kitchener's Army with enthusiasm but soon found the conduct of the war to be contrary to his Quaker beliefs. He joined the Friends' War Victims' Relief Committee, working in France, building temporary accommodation and helping on the farms. He was granted exemption from military service, probably because the Prefect of the Marne sent a statement to the Salisbury Tribunal confirming that his work was important in raising French morale. It would appear that there was considerable co-operation between the French and the English at this level. Colonel Lord Radnor, on his return from India, was appointed Director of Agricultural Production in France which meant that he was responsible for organising the cultivation of some 60,000 acres behind the allied forces' lines.

A baker in the local asylum claimed exemption, stating that if a substitute was found he would have to work with lunatics which might not be everyone's cup of tea.

A remarkably confused domain; some applications for exemption verged on the comic, as with the fish and chip shop proprietor in Salisbury who was excused military service on the grounds that he was sustaining morale in the city and thereby performing a national service.

Eighty cases came before the Salisbury Rural Tribunal at the council chamber in April 1918. Some of the proceedings were recorded by the *Journal* as follows:

'In the case of the head carter on a farm at Stratford Toney, 30, single and passed for general service, the employer stated that he supported his widowed mother. Thirty-five acres had been ploughed up this spring on the farm making eighty acres altogether… .'

Mr Livens (National Service Representative): "If the military could find you an equally good head carter would you release this young man?"

Employer: "I would."

The Chairman pointed out that if married men of 30 were going to be sent to the army, the Tribunal could hardly exempt single young men.

Mr Waters (another Board member) said that this man's

employer did a lot of public work, and had recently been placed on the County Wages Committee, which would take up much more of his time. Men who did public work must have good men on their farms, or else food production would suffer. If this employer had a soldier substitute sent him who did not understand the work there would be decreased production.

Mr Livens said that he recognised the great value of this man but it was obvious to the Tribunal that he was required for military service. The two interests had to be adjusted.

The Tribunal allowed an exemption until October 11th, but the Chairman said they hoped that a substitute would be found.'

Surely, an extended exemption must have felt like a suspended death sentence.

'Exemption was asked for a milker who lived at Coombe Bisset, 20, single...
The National Service Department reported that they could not assent to any exemption.
Mr Livens thought the District Council should liberate roadmen to replace essential young men on farms.
Mr Harding (another Board member): "Roadmen don't milk".
Mr Livens: "Some of them can. We press this for this man, out of hand".
Final exemption to May 15th was given.'

Press? Why does this conversation remind me of one that might have occurred in a harbour pub during the Napoleonic wars?

'A Homington Farm manager, 19, single....for whom exemption was asked, stated that during the illness of his grandfather (the occupier) he was carrying on the farm of 170 acres. He did all the buying and selling, kept the accounts and drew the cheques. He was given until October 11th.'

Complications also arose for long-serving, self-employed business men. In June 1918 the tradesmen of Salisbury and district requested Charles Bathurst to present a question in the House of Commons as to why sole traders of some twenty years who were also employers should be treated differently, with regard to exemption, to 'insurance and bank clerks, newspaper compositors, blacksmiths, brick makers and other work people of the same age.'

A somewhat nebulous answer came back from the Minister, confirming that the matter was under consideration.

Returning to the tribunal, further matters were also under review:

> *'An application for a renewed exemption of a Downton doctor's chauffeur (45, married) was assented to by the National Service authorities if a substitute could not be found.*
>
> *The employer's wife said that it was particularly necessary that her husband should have a chauffeur at the present time, when his work was particularly hard. They had made efforts to get a substitute but had been unsuccessful. They could not get any labour now, let alone a chauffeur.*
>
> *Mr Baglin (another Board member) said that he had brought the case before headquarters with a view to getting a substitute, but had heard nothing about it since.*
>
> *The Chairman: "The Doctor has obviously done his best. He cannot do more."*
>
> *Mr Baglin: "It would not be possible to get a female to drive?"*
>
> *Employer's wife: "I don't think under the circumstances he would be comfortable with one."*
>
> *The Tribunal granted an exemption for four months, until March 1st.*
>
> *Mr Shears (another Board member): "We hope the war will be over by then."*
>
> *Mr Harding: "We all hope that."'*

Immersed in material published in 1918, I undoubtedly began to detect a whiff of optimism. Surely, it was felt that the war could not last much longer. On 3 April, following the launch of the German Spring Offensive on 21 March, the Allied forces on the Western Front were united under Marshal Foch, to meet an attack that was *'unparalleled in its concentration of troops and guns'*. The *Journal* continued in its leader: *'this secures, for the first time, efficient unity of action and co-*

Soldiers and Scouts parade in the Market Place on Empire Day, 1918.
(Wiltshire and Swindon History Centre)

ordination of effort, and cannot fail to have far-reaching results upon the vast struggle ... .' Lloyd George, not immune from hyperbole, called the ensuing battle, 'the greatest battle ever fought in the history of the world.' No wonder the casualties were so high.

On Empire Day (24 May) there was the customary parade in the Market Place with flag waving children and all the usual symbols of loyalty to the Crown and Empire. Three hundred soldiers – one major and the remainder NCOs – were decorated: mostly from the Dominions, some from the United Kingdom but none from the Wiltshire Regiment who were on active service.

The German advance was halted at the Marne in July. Was this, truly, the beginning of the end? Less good news came with the sinking, by a German torpedo, of RMS *Carpathia*, the Cunard liner that had picked up survivors from the *Titanic* in 1912. Fortunately, there were few fatalities.

As was customary at the *Journal*, their pages were peppered with international news. In July 1918, Salisbury folk were treated to a scathing attack on the Tsar, whose murder had just been announced.

'...where it is impossible not to pity the miserable end of Nicholas II, the revelations of the last two years have effectively destroyed the feelings of respect which Europe formerly entertained for him...as a ruler Nicholas II was an extraordinary mixture of sinister qualities. It is not improbable that he meant well even when he did evil.'

The paper did, however, concede that *'a more horrible crime is not recorded in history'*, when referring specifically to the murder of the Tsarevich by the Bolsheviks.

Under less violent political skies, reforms were under way in Britain with the passing of the Franchise Bill: 1918. In Salisbury, the old 'City' constituency was merged with 'South Wilts' and Godfrey Locker-Lampson was forced to seek a parliamentary seat elsewhere. He wrote to the *Journal*: *'I cannot but be deeply sorry that the old historic Parliamentary Borough with so much distinguished history behind it, should come to an end.'*

Charles Bathurst (South Wilts) was soon to be elevated to the Lords where, as Lord Bledisloe, he would speak on behalf of the Ministry of Food. He took his name from the ancient Bledeslowe Hundred where his estates were located on the banks of the Severn Estuary. The winds of political change were blowing in Wiltshire. In October, Hugh Morrison was elected as prospective Coalition member of the re-constituted constituency. His brother had been Member for South Wilts from 1899–1906.

As harvest time approached and news of the war became ever more hopeful, even public school boys appeared in the fields to provide assistance, although Eva Sillence, writing from Wiltshire to relations in New York, complains of the damage inflicted by mid-summer frosts, particularly on plums and strawberries. Meanwhile, a traction-engine driver was granted exemption from military service and the local agent advertised in Salisbury for the new Massey-Harris, farm equipment. Mr C.H.E. Chubb, who had bought Stonehenge earlier in the decade, gave it to the nation with the proviso that any revenue, during the remainder of the war, should be donated to the Red Cross.

Nevertheless, recruiting kept up apace. Queen Mary's Army Auxiliary Corps advertised for clerks, cooks and waitresses *'for service at home or overseas'* and there was little let up in the casualties.

A few months before the end of the war, the *Journal* stated that '*every business house in Salisbury should have its Roll of Honour displayed in the shop or office, showing the number of employees who have joined the colours.*' The paper provided a service whereby '*artistically printed*' specimens could be selected at their office.

During the last few months of 1918 the deaths of two young men received particular attention in the *Journal*.

> '*Rifleman Benjamin Bucknall who had been gassed but remained in the field until he had discharged his supply of ammunition – "letting the Boches have the full 200 rounds" – as he later wrote to a friend, was himself killed by machine gun fire.*'

Roll of Honour.

EVERY Business House in Salisbury should have its ROLL OF HONOUR displayed in the Shop or Office, showing the names and number of Employés who have joined the Colours.

They are artistically printed, and specimens may be seen at the "JOURNAL" OFFICE, Canal, Salisbury.

He had trained as an architect with Mr Fred Bath of Salisbury. The *Journal* reported that '*he quickly made headway in his profession, and at the time of joining was very proficient, for one so young, his drawings showed exceptional merit... .*'

The death of Captain Cuthbert Hodding, the son of the town clerk and who had been educated at Marlborough College also received considerable notice. He had been articled to Messrs Hodding and Jackson, solicitors of Salisbury, before acting as managing clerk to solicitors in Oxford and Reading. He had been an enthusiastic hockey player who played centre half-back for the West of England.

As the autumn leaves turned russet in the parks and open spaces that surround Salisbury Cathedral the possibility of an early Armistice seemed ever more likely. Peace notes were flying between Washington and Berlin, although the London *Times* described the German approach as a '*monument of insincerity, make belief and deliberate untruth*'. On the ground, significant events were occurring. The Bulgarians were routed and sued for peace in late September and on the Western Front

The open spaces that surround Salisbury Cathedral today (2015). (NGMH)

the German defence system known as the Hindenburg Line was breached. On 19 October the *Journal* commenced its leader with the words *'since our last issue events have moved with dramatic swiftness'*. Eleven days later an Armistice was signed with Turkey.

On 9 November the *Journal* reported the following:

> *'The following wireless message was transmitted to the German High Command by Marshal Foch: "If the German Plenipotentiaries wish to meet Marshal Foch to ask for an Armistice they are to advance to the Front outposts by the Chimey Fourmies – La Capelle – Guise Road. Orders have been given that they are to be received and conducted to the place fixed for the interview."'*

On the same day the leader stated that *'this week has been filled with events momentous in the history of civilisation'*, and went on to announce the unconditional surrender of the Austro-Hungarian Empire.

A week later the *Journal* informed readers, as they sat at their breakfast tables, about something they probably already knew. For those who had survived, and there would have been few that were not scarred, reading of the assassination of the Archduke Franz Ferdinand in Sarajevo must have seemed a very long time ago.

> *'The war has ended as suddenly as it began. On Monday the terms of the Armistice, laid down by the Associated Powers were accepted by the German Plenipotentiaries and at eleven o'clock on the morning of that day, November 11th, all military operations by land and in the air ceased.'*

Huge demonstrations and crowds revelling and dancing filled the streets of Salisbury during the week following the Armistice. The Scots Guards played in the Market Square and the clock tower in Fisherton Street was illuminated for the first time since 1914. A fleet of more than forty planes wheeled and circled over the city and a general holiday was granted to the Australian troops who poured into the city along with others, probably New Zealanders and Americans.

The mayor, standing on a hastily constructed platform in front of the council chamber, accompanied by the mayoress and several dignitaries, remarked that he could hardly speak because his heart was too full for words. The only comment he felt he could make was to say 'thank God the war is over.' A Thanksgiving Service was arranged for Sunday, 17 November in the Cathedral.

Writing in *Bishop Wordsworth's School 1890–1950*, a past student recorded her memories of the day:

> *'I remember how on Armistice Day, Monsieur Hellman, half-crying, half-laughing in his excitement, burst into our classroom shouting, "It's over! It's over!" Quickly reacting, we leapt up and were preparing to dash out, to feel very crushed when the unruffled voice of our mistress told us to sit down and proceed with the next sentence!'*

And, indeed, practical matters required attention. The urgent return of prisoners and the wounded was a priority and the press was soon full of recriminations as to how prisoners had been treated in Germany and Turkey.

T.E. Lawrence, it would appear – although this is a controversial issue – was not the only one to have been abused.

According to Richard Broadhead's book, *Salisbury Soldiers*, fourteen members of the military were killed or died of wounds or illness after Armistice Day and before the end of the year. The last soldier, from the region, to be killed in action, was Major Henry Farrer MC, the second son of Canon and Mrs Farrer of The Close, Salisbury. But how many more would continue to die from the effects of the conflict? Such a question is impossible to answer although Juliet Nicolson addresses the topic in some detail in her book *The Great Silence*. In *Public Schools and the Great War* a photograph features George Howson, the headmaster of Gresham's with his prefects in 1918. The caption reads: '*Howson died in January 1919 – the war killed him as surely as if he had fallen at the Front.*'

The new 'buzz' word was 'reconstruction'. Lady Hulse, speaking to pupils and staff at The Godolphin School, praised the efforts made during the war and 'urged that they should give their highest and best for England….in the days of reconstruction that are to come.' However, to my surprise, she added that she did not believe in the League of Nations because it was 'against human nature…for certain nations to manage others'.

The headmaster of Bishop Wordsworth's School spoke of boys and girls who were prepared 'to take their place and do their part in building up the new England' and H. Case, the furnishers of Fisherton Street, advertised their wares with the rider: '*The Great Age of Reconstruction is about to commence… .*'

Striking a more trivial note, Lord Bledisloe's first act was to increase the sugar allowance for children and the sick and wounded. A Peace Christmas or Victory Christmas was on the horizon, after all! Safely ensconced in the House of Lords he would escape the turmoil of the General Election on 14 December when women would vote for the first time and the Coalition (Liberals/Conservatives) was returned with David Lloyd George remaining as Prime Minister.

This was also a time for thanks as illustrated by this letter to Queen Mary's Needlework Guild and signed Corporal C. Hold – 'With the British Expeditionary Force.'

'Dear Miss Baker
I wish to thank you very much for the parcel I received from
Queen Mary's Needlework Guild. I have been on active service
since October 1916 and must say that your parcel is absolutely
the best I have seen sent to France. It contains everything a
soldier needs. It is certainly most splendid work of your Guild
and I appreciate it very much again. Thanking you and your
many good workers and I also send heartiest good wishes and
merry Christmas to you all wishing you every success.'

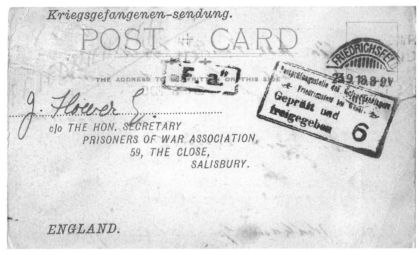

A form sent by Private William Taylor of the Wiltshire Regiment, a prisoner
of war at Friedrichsfeld, acknowledging a parcel of food in good condition.
'F.a.' stands for 'Frist Abgelaufen' and indicates that a period of official delay
(imposed so that any hidden messages would no longer be useful) had expired.
(T.S. Crawford)

As the New Year approached a huge advertisement appeared in the newspapers. It announced that the Red Lion Hotel of Milford Street, Salisbury, which dates back to the thirteenth century when it was reputed to have been established to house the craftsmen and masons building the cathedral, had been completely re-decorated and served a special luncheon on Market Days.

The War to End all Wars was, indeed, over.

The Red Lion in Milford Street, Salisbury as it is today – a Best Western Hotel (2015). (NGMH)

Onward and upward!

However, in her fascinating book, *Child of the Red Lion*, Molly Maidment, who was born in the hotel that her parents owned in 1917, and who remained involved with life in that most excellent establishment until her death in 1992, records a vignette, that to my mind encapsulates the bitter-sweet days that immediately followed the Great War:

'By the age of four I knew a lot about the Great War. We lived in its aftermath and one of the most dramatic happenings of my early life was something called GOING OVER THE TOP. There was a porter, Ginger, who served in the trenches for four long years and he kept me enthralled with endless stories of his wartime exploits. Ginger's wife was stone-deaf so he was glad to have me as a willing listener who never tired of his stories of Hill 60. Occasionally, when he drank too much he donned his helmet and with his knapsack thrown over his trench coat he crawled up the main stairs on all fours yelling that he was GOING OVER THE TOP to get "those bloody Jerries". He taught me to sing "It's a Long Way to Tipperary" and "Pack Up Your Troubles" and I was soon word perfect in various versions of "Mademoiselle From Armentières", much to the disgust of Nanny. Sometimes when he was crying drunk I would weep with Ginger for all his lost comrades, for his lost youth and for the agony and anguish of his four horrific years in the trenches.'

CHAPTER 6

1919

'When the long trek is over...'

'When the long trek is over,
And the last long trench filled in,
I'll take a boat to Dover,
Away from all the din;
I'll take a trip to Mendip,
I'll see the Wiltshire downs,
And all my soul I'll then dip
In peace no trouble drowns.

Away from the noise of battle,
Away from bombs and shells,
I'll lie where browse the cattle,
Or pluck the purple bells.
I'll lie among the heather,
And watch the distant plain,
Through all the summer weather,
Nor go to fight again.'

Poor Alec de Candole, who was educated at Marlborough College, never found the peace he sought on this earth. Two days after writing these lines, in September 1918, he was killed in a bombing raid on German trenches.

Many sought peace and fulfilment after the Armistice but found themselves in a very new world. In the early months of 1919 there was even the constant threat of renewed hostilities and the slow path to demobilisation caused considerable dissatisfaction. Lloyd George found it necessary to remind the nation that 'although the fighting has stopped the war is not over. The German armies have not been demobilised and are still very powerful.' The Germans only ratified the Treaty of Versailles two hours before the November Armistice was due to expire, protesting against 'the unheard of injustice of the conditions of peace' and declaring that they only concurred because the German people no longer had the means to defend themselves. Signed on 28 June 1919, exactly five years after the assassination of the Archduke, was it, indeed, a renewed Armistice for twenty years as has been noted by some historians?

There were considerable delays in demobilisation and in one instance a mutiny of 'Derby Men' occurred on the Plain because they were under the misapprehension that the Armistice had concluded the war and that they were free men. What to do with men released from the forces was also a conundrum. Proposals were drawn up to settle former officers and men on the land with small holdings.

Of all the effects of the war, few are easier to identify than the burning sense of loyalty and comradeship that had grown up between those who had served in such dreadful conditions and so the Salisbury Branch of the Comrades of the Great War was founded. The purpose of the Comrades was 'to draw together all those who have had the honour to serve their God, King and Country.... '

Many Belgians returned to their war-torn country and Institutions that had fulfilled their purpose well during the war, such as VAD Hospitals, Queen Mary's Needlework Guild and The Salisbury Guest House – a popular rendezvous for soldiers – were wound up and closed.

In January 1919, despite the continued anxiety relating to the food supply, a massive banquet was held in the Salisbury Council House for 150 returned prisoners of war. The company stood in silence and raised their glasses – 'to the memory of their comrades who would never reach their homeland again.'

Back on the Plain at Shrewton, the prosperous Chant family, where Ethel would be seven years old in February 1919, had been eagerly awaiting the return of her uncle Albert, who had been conscripted into the 6th Battalion of the Wiltshire Regiment in May 1916. Detailed

Formerly occupied by solicitors Harding and Hall, this property provided a place of solace for soldiers during the Great War. (Peter Daniels)

A reception was given for one hundred and eighty guests at the Council House in January 1919. Most of the party were returned prisoners of war and Mayor James Macklin presented each man with a silver-plated cigarette case. (Peter Daniels)

SALISBURY'S WELCOME
RETURNED
PRISONERS OF WAR
JANUARY 23ᵗ 1919

Bakers at H.L. Chant's Supply Stores in Shrewton at the beginning of the Great War. Albert Chant is seated, second from left. (Ken Jones)

records no longer exist but Albert had met his brother, Louis, briefly at the front in early 1918. It was the last time any member of the family would see him as he was captured by the Germans in March, probably during Operation Michael, and sent to work on a farm. His wife, Louisa, received a letter from him in October saying that he was as well as could be expected in the circumstances. Nevertheless, he apparently died of influenza shortly afterwards. It would be many frustrating months, when his family expected his cheery face to appear at the bake-house door at any time, before the family heard of his demise and received his death certificate, signed by the Burgomaster of Niederzissen and dated 27 June 1919. Shortly afterwards the following appeared in the *Journal*.

> '*CHANT. – In ever loving memory of Private A.V. Chant, the dearly-loved husband of Louisa Chant, who passed away November 1st 1918, whilst a prisoner of war in Germany.*
> *All is dark within our dwelling,*
> *Lonely is our home today,*
> *A loving husband and a daddy dear*
> *From this earth has passed away.*'

Those that were left of our friends from the Empire and United States were soon packing their bags and returning home, some taking English brides with them. The casualties had been awesome, although the Canadian, Lieutenant Harry Colebourn had survived. He returned to the London Zoo to collect his treasured bear, Winnie. However, finding that she had become so well behaved, tame and much loved he decided to leave her in the care of her keepers. In 1924, A.A. Milne visited the zoo with his son, Christopher Robin who became enchanted with Winnie. Two years later Milne, having changed the bear's gender, published the first Winnie-the-Pooh book.

Many who had crossed oceans in the defence of the Empire remained, silent, in graveyards across Wiltshire. Echoing a famous epitaph – *'si monumentum requiris circumspice'*[2]– in some cases regimental badges were carved on the Plain's chalk down lands. British, Australian and New Zealand units all left their marks, such as the 'Bulford Kiwi' above Sling Camp. Soldiers in the Fovant area created almost forty badges and unit titles on the hillside above their camps, many of the less-impressive examples soon disappearing under vegetation and from erosion. Today the surviving badges are maintained by the Fovant Badges Society. One in six men who had trained on Salisbury Plain lost their lives and many others were left physically maimed or mentally scarred.

Kiwi Emblem cut out of chalk by the New Zealand forces to commemorate their occupation of Sling Camp, Bulford, during the Great War. (T.S. Crawford)

2 'If you seek his monument look around', the inscription on the tomb of Sir Christopher Wren in St Paul's Cathedral.

Salisbury, the surrounding region and the nation must have had to shake itself violently to adjust to what we would describe today as the 'new normal'. War- time relationships needed to be sorted out. In many cases, as has been so often recorded, those who had returned from the war zones were changed men and did not want – or were not able - to discuss their experiences. R.F. Delderfield's *To Serve Them All My Days* is such a good book in this respect. For the first time, many women had experienced a certain freedom and their own money and the first lady councillor – the delightfully named, Mrs Cowmeadow of St Ann Street – was elected to the City Council. Also, in Salisbury, Woodrow and Co. of Castle Street placed a large advertisement, offering to supply '*Baby Carriages*' and we know – my own mother was born in 1919 – exactly what that meant.

Slowly, step by step, the twin aspects of memory and renewal encompassed life in Salisbury and the surrounding regions. Committees were set up in most villages to decide on the appropriate forms of memorial to the fallen as can be witnessed today by stone crosses or other edifices in countless churchyards or on numerous village greens.

Five thousand members of the Wiltshire Regiment had lost their lives between 1914 and 1918. A memorial hall was planned in Salisbury, to honour those citizens who had made the final sacrifice, but was rejected in favour of an elaborate war memorial that was

Memorial to the Old Contemptibles Association in St Mary's Church, Breamore. (NGMH)

constructed in the Market Square at a cost of £2,500. In the presence of the Bishop of Salisbury and other dignitaries, it was unveiled on Sunday, 12 February 1922 by Lieutenant Tom Edwin Adlam VC and dedicated by the Rev R.F. Addison VC. To appropriate Sassoon's words in his poem '*Aftermath*': '*the world's events had rumbled on since those gagged days, like traffic checked awhile at the crossing of city ways.*'

The memorial which features the names of 461 of the fallen still dominates the Market Square today. The Cathedral itself holds few reminders of the war. There are the wooden crosses in the cloisters which, shipped from the front, once marked the immediate resting place of six officers and Gunner G.A.K. Buskin of the Australian Imperial Force; and the chapels of St Laurence and St Michael the Archangel in the south transept, feature memorial windows. In the latter the Diocesan Book of Remembrance is displayed together with memorials to the Duke of Edinburgh's Royal Regiment, Bishop F.E. Ridgeway (1911–1921) and fifty eight members of the Salisbury Diocesan Guild of Ringers and other ringers who had never returned to toll their peals across the broad chalk lands and river valleys of

The Salisbury War Memorial in the Market Place, unveiled by Lieutenant Edwin Adlam VC in 1922. The inscription reads: 'In Honour and Remembrance of the Citizens of Salisbury who Served. Who Fought. Who Died. For Freedom, Hope and Humanity: 1914-1919.' (Peter Daniels)

Salisbury Cathedral: memorial to those members of the Salisbury Diocesan Guild of Ringers who died in the Great War. (NGMH)

Salisbury Cathedral: memorial to the choristers of the Cathedral and other members of the Cathedral School who fell in the World Wars of 1914-1918 and 1939-1945. (NGMH)

Wiltshire. Following further research it is planned that an additional Book of Remembrance will be opened recording the names of more ringers who fell in the conflict. The Royal Berkshire and Wiltshire Regiments were amalgamated in 1959 as The Duke of Edinburgh's Royal Regiment. The names of numerous Great War battles, which were awarded as battle honours to the regiment, are emblazoned on the colours. These were laid up in the Cathedral in 1987.

In the chancel, the names of thirteen members of the Salisbury choristers and Cathedral school are recorded on a small but elaborate memorial and elsewhere individual plaques record several fallen heroes. These include Lieutenant Edward Wyndham Tennant, the son of a former Salisbury MP, Lord Glenconner, who was killed on the Somme and of whom one soldier wrote: '*When things were at their worst, he would pass up and down the trench cheering the men...When danger was greatest, his smile was loveliest.*'

In the south aisle there is a memorial to Jacob Pleydell-Bouverie, 6th Earl of Radnor, who had also been a local MP and Lord Lieutenant of Wiltshire – it was placed there in 1930 by his widow, who had supervised the war time hospital at Longford Castle so tirelessly, and her ten children.

Shortly after the war, James Macklin was appointed Deputy Lieutenant of the County of Wiltshire and a knighthood followed in the New Year Honours in 1920. He received this accolade, for his public and local services, from King George V at Buckingham Palace in 1920, the year before he received the Freedom of the City of Salisbury. A handsome man, his portrait hangs in the council chamber. He continued to serve the city, as alderman, for a further twenty years and died in 1944 aged 79. His wife, Barbara, received the Order of the British Empire for work

James Macklin – Mayor of Salisbury, 1913-1919. (Salisbury City Council)

with the troops during the Great War and the Golden Palms of the Order of the Crown by the King of the Belgians for work with refugees during the conflict. She died in 1960 aged 89.

Other notable characters who had played a significant role in Salisbury life during the tumultuous war years include Lord Bledisloe who soared upwards with his career, becoming a member of the Privy Council in 1926 and serving as Governor General of New Zealand from 1930-1935. He died, aged ninety in 1958 at Lydney, his estate in Gloucestershire.

Godfrey Locker-Lampson's advancement also led to his becoming a Privy Counsellor (1928) and in the same year he became a member of the British Delegation to the League of Nations in Geneva. He was a published poet and historian and died in 1946 aged seventy.

The *Journal* of early 1919 records individual items that reflect a city trying to get back on its feet – although one might discount the cases of bigamy that came up at the assizes! Hunting appointments were as numerous as ever, drinking licenses were renewed and cricket and other sporting plans were restored. Women's football aroused some controversy. In some regions it was considered vulgar and unsuitable that women, – many were now no longer employed – should continue with the sport and in 1921 the Football Association banned their members from allowing women to use their grounds.

The Silver Grill at the Haunch of Venison was re-opened and a row developed concerning the lopping of beautiful old elms in the Close. Across the green, the Bishop admonished his flock for falling behind in confirmation instruction for the young and at the Infirmary plans were implemented to reduce the beds which had served some 3,000 military personnel during the conflict. In the weekly minutes of the hospital's management committee, where records of the Spanish Influenza are remarkably sparse, concern was expressed as to who would be providing '*a shaving and haircutting service*', for the few remaining wounded now that the wartime voluntary arrangements had ceased. A request was also made for a typewriter '*for the military correspondence*' and a Remington No. 7 was purchased for sixteen guineas.

Country estates continued to suffer from lack of manpower and city businesses, no doubt, struggled to adapt to a new and soldierless world. Those entering the Close today might be intrigued to see a white

The building that housed the Infirmary in Salisbury – now converted to flats (2015). (NGMH)

wooden ram perched above the entrance to a hairdressers. The ram commemorates the site of the retail outlet for the Stonehenge Woollen Industries, a business, well established before the Great War whose weavers included several cut down in their service to King and Empire. However the firm continued in business until 1959.

Perhaps one of the saddest stories is that of Scout Motors. Following the cessation of car production in 1915 and the transfer of many skilled workers to other centres in the United Kingdom and even to France, it was well into 1920 before production had recommenced in Salisbury. Even then, delayed payments for government contracts, strikes, huge increases in the cost of raw materials, demands for new designs and increased competition provided a stranglehold over the re-birth of the business. Morris Cowley, amongst other manufacturers, opened showrooms in Salisbury. Suddenly, the end was nigh and following

"SCOUT" MOTOR AMBULANCE   19.6. H.P.

Scout

WITH OBSCURED WINDOWS, 2 STRETCHERS PLACED IN POSITION THROUGH DOOR AT BACK. STEEL INTERCHANGEABLE WHEELS.

Scout Motor Ambulance. (Peter Daniels)

court proceedings for a relatively small debt (£112) the company was wound up in the summer of 1921.

Amongst the wreckage and the opportunities that faced the British population during the early post-war years were those who tried to come to terms with what had happened to their loved ones. Rudyard Kipling and his wife, as has been well documented, continued to search for their son, *My Boy Jack*, who was almost certainly killed at the battle of Loos in 1915, and did not finally acknowledge that he was lost for many years. Sir Arthur Conan Doyle, whose son, Kingsley, had been wounded at the Somme and died of influenza in 1918 pursued a spiritualist path as did many citizens in Wiltshire. The *Journal* advertised lectures relating to '*Man's Life after Death*' under the heading of '*Spiritualism*'. Many died of grief and many more endeavoured to live life, of a sort, after the war.

Two and a half million war veterans, countrywide, continued to receive a disability pension for years to come and Second World War baby boomers, such as myself, will recall that the maimed and gassed were still in evidence – many in ungainly and unwieldy invalid carriages – on city streets in the fifties and early sixties.

In conclusion, and more heartening, is a passage I came across in *Witness* (1962), the autobiography of the industrialist, author and mystic, John Godolphin Bennett, who is buried at Sparkford, on the Wiltshire-Somerset border. A former soldier on the Western Front, he is describing a visit to his old school (KCS: Wimbledon} when he sees the names of the fallen on a monument:

'*I knew why I had never returned: I had never reconciled myself to the loss of so many of my best friends. I was all alone on the great playing field; but, as I stood, I was no longer alone. All these boys were still there; still living with their powers undiminished... An immense joy flooded through me. Past all understanding, it was yet true that premature death is not necessarily a disaster. Potentialities are not destroyed by death.*'

Salisbury Cathedral from the gardens of Bishop Wordsworth's School as it is today (2015). (NGMH)

Bibliography

Published books, poems and pamphlets read as general interest and research material in the writing of this book:

1913: The year Before the Storm, Florian Illies, Clerkenwell Press
A Century in Shrewton, Ken and Elizabeth Jones
An English Baby Boomer: My Life and Times, Neil G.M. Hall, Muncaster Press
Aftermath, Siegfried Sassoon
Aviation in Wiltshire, Norman C. Parker and South Wiltshire Industrial Archaeology Department
Bishop Wordsworth's School 1890-1950, F.C. Happold, (Privately printed for Bishop Wordsworth's School, Salisbury, 1950)
Child of the Red Lion, Molly Maidment, Red Lion Publications
In the Shadow of Salisbury Spire, Peter L. Smith, the Hobnob Press
Letters: written from the English Front in France between September 1914 and March 1915 by Captain Sir Edward Hamilton Westrow Hulse Bt
Peace and War, Britain in 1914, Nigel Jones, Head of Zeus
Poems and drawings, Sister Mabel Myring
Public Schools and the Great War, Anthony Seldon and David Walsh, Pen and Sword
Scout Motors of Salisbury 1902-1921, Jim Watkinson and South Wiltshire Industrial Archaeology Society
The Canadian Army on Salisbury Plain, T.S. Crawford, Halsgrove
The First World War and its Impact on Salisbury, Ruth Newman
The Godolphin School 1726-1926, M.A. Douglas and C.R. Ash, Longmans, Green and Co
The Godolphin School Magazine 1917-1922

The Great War: Salisbury Soldiers, Richard Broadhead, Tempus Publishing

The Great Silence, Juliet Nicolson, John Murray

The Hospital Barge, Wilfred Owen

The Kitchen is the Key to Victory, Christine Ball, Nicky Hudson and West Sussex County Council

The Marlburian 1917 (Marlborough College)

The Nestlé Company in Salisbury, John Pothecary and South Wiltshire Industrial Archaeology Society

The Salisbury and Winchester Journal

The White Hart, Don Cross, Wessexplore

The Wiltshire Regiment 1914-1959, Martin McIntyre, Tempus Publishing

Three Generations, Norman Thorne

Wiltshire and the Great War, T.S. Crawford, the Crowood Press

Witness, John G. Bennett, Hodder and Stoughton

Hansard (1916)

Peace, Rupert Brooke

Punch

The Times Literary Supplement (1909)

The World Crisis, Winston S. Churchill

NB

Breamore House – this Elizabethan Manor House near Salisbury, is the residence of the Hulse family and is open to the public on certain days during the summer. A tour of the house and visit to the museum should not be missed!

Lydney Park – the residence of the current Lord Bledisloe in Gloucestershire is open to the public annually, in the spring, on designated days. The gardens are splendid and well worth a visit.

Tidworth is a garrison town in Wiltshire and from 1916 was the headquarters of the Australian Imperial Force

The Tedworth Hunt is the local Wiltshire pack of foxhounds.

Wilton House – the residence of the 18th Earl of Pembroke is open to the public on certain days and for special events.

Index